MODERN JAPAN

UNIFORM WITH THIS BOOK

RONALD HINGLEY *Russian Revolution*

RICHARD PROCKTOR *Nazi Germany*

LOIS MITCHISON *Chinese Revolution*

IN PREPARATION

LOIS MITCHISON *The Indian Nations*

A BODLEY HEAD CONTEMPORARY HISTORY

MODERN JAPAN

RICHARD SIMS

THE BODLEY HEAD

LONDON SYDNEY
TORONTO

ACKNOWLEDGMENTS

Thanks are due to the following for permission to reproduce copyright photographs: The Japan Information Centre, London, pages 6, 12, 15, 21, 36, 43, 98, 106; Tokyo National Museum, page 19; The Japan Cultural Society, Tokyo, pages 28, 34, 38, 48, 50, 51, 53, 54, 60, 62, 66, 68, 73, 76; The Trustees of the British Museum, pages 24 and 46; The Imperial War Musuem, pages 79, 86, 87; the Kyodo News Service, Tokyo, page 88; Fox Photos Limited, page 93; *Japan Times*, Tokyo, page 100; Keystone Press Agency, page 105.

Maps © The Bodley Head Ltd 1973
ISBN 0 370 01567 3
Printed and bound in Great Britain for
The Bodley Head Ltd
9 Bow Street, London WC2E 7AL
by Cox & Wyman Ltd, Fakenham
Set in Monophoto Baskerville
First published 1973

CONTENTS

1. The Historical Background, 7
2. Traditional Society, 14
3. The End of Isolation, 26
4. The Samurai Revolution, 30
5. The Meiji Oligarchs, 37
6. Economic Modernisation, 45
7. The New Society of Meiji Japan, 52
8. Taishō Japan, 58
9. Japan in World Politics (1905–30), 64
10. Crisis at Home and Abroad, 69
11. The Triumph of Militarism, 75
12. The Pacific War, 80
13. Japan under Occupation, 91
14. Contemporary Japan, 97

Books for further reading, 109
Index, 110

1

The Historical Background

Few developments in modern history have been more dramatic than Japan's transformation during the last hundred years. In the mid-nineteenth century the Japanese islands might have vanished from the map without the greater part of the outside world being in any way affected, or even aware. Yet within two generations Japan had inflicted defeat on Imperial Russia and a few decades later she was to challenge the might of America and create a vast, if short-lived, East Asian empire.

Today Japan has risen from military humiliation to become the world's third largest industrial power. Her growth rate has averaged over ten per cent since the 1950s and predictions have been made that by the 1990s the Japanese will have the highest per capita income level of any nation.

This transformation has produced an image of Japan as a highly modern state, comparable with the leading countries of the West rather than those of Asia. Yet no one who has lived in Japan can be unaware of the survival of many distinctive traditions from the past. When Japan was forcibly introduced into the international community in the 1850s, she possessed a proud heritage not lightly to be abandoned or thrust aside. Many Japanese, while accepting modernisation in some areas of life, clung to tradition in others. To understand modern Japan, therefore, it is important to know something of her geographical, historical and social background.

7

◀ Old and new in the Japanese landscape. The juxtaposition of Japan's
most famous mountain, Fuji, and a modern highway symbolises
the co-existence of traditional and modern in present-day Japan

Japan is made up of a large number of islands, of which the chief are Honshū, Kyūshū, Shikoku, and Hokkaidō, but although Hokkaidō reaches as far north as Montreal and Kyūshū lies on the same latitude as Israel, the total area is less than 150,000 square miles, making Japan larger than Britain but smaller than France. Compared with China, her chief neighbour, Japan is a midget.

Less than one-sixth of Japan's land is suitable for cultivation. Most of the country is densely wooded hillside and mountain, spectacular in its beauty, but economically of limited value. Japan's position on the edge of the monsoon region, however, has made highly productive rice cultivation possible, and the Japanese islands are surrounded by rich fishing grounds. Against this, there are no great rivers which can be used for travel or large-scale irrigation, and earthquakes are frequent. The most famous occurred in 1923, in the Tōkyō–Yokohama area, and caused the loss of an estimated 132,807 lives and 576,262 houses.

Perhaps the most significant geographical fact, however, is that Japan is separated from the Asian continent by a broad and dangerous stretch of water. Korea, her nearest neighbour, is 115 miles from Kyūshū, more than five times the distance between Britain and Europe.

Before the 1939–45 war the Japanese were officially taught that their country was created by the gods and that, about 3,000 years ago, Ninigi, a grandson of the sun goddess, descended from heaven to rule over it. This myth, deriving from eighth-century writings, was often combined with an assumption that every Japanese family was a branch family of the main imperial family and that Japan therefore enjoyed a unique racial purity. It was not until the post-war years that these official fabrications were openly criticised. Since 1945, however, archaeologists have pushed back the story of Japan's habitation to a much earlier period, and it has been established that there was a gradual influx of migrants into Japan from several directions rather than one invasion from a particular area.

This diversity of racial origin is hardly surprising, for before 20,000 BC there were land links with the Asian continent both to the north and the south. Indeed, there is evidence that hunters may have lived in Japan 250,000 years ago. The first culture with a knowledge of pottery, however, did not begin until about 5,000 BC, and agriculture was not known until the third century BC, when it was brought from Korea. Nevertheless, despite these connections with the Asian continent, no large-scale invasions have disturbed the established pattern since the first Japanese state emerged in

Yamato in west central Japan in the third century AD. By the fourth century all the inhabitants of Japan, except the Ainu of northern Japan and other minor unassimilated groups, were speaking the same language and sharing the same basic culture.

The Yamato dynasty steadily extended its sway over the rest of Japan, but it is unlikely that it would have continued to reign in unbroken line

MODERN JAPAN

down to the present day if it had not taken the momentous step of introducing Chinese culture and Chinese methods of government. Beginning with the introduction of Buddhism in the late sixth century, the process of borrowing reached a political climax in the Taika Reform, proclaimed in 646. Among its aims were the establishment of a centralised bureaucratic government; the erection of a permanent capital; and the take-over by the imperial government of all cultivated land. By the end of the eighth century, Japan had an impressive capital in Heian (now Kyōto), an effective government, and an incomparably higher cultural level.

It was, indeed, in the field of culture that Japan owed her greatest debt to China. Apart from official missions sent to the T'ang court between 607 and 838, there was a constant flow of unofficial visitors to China, particularly Buddhist priests. The latter not only returned to Japan with religious ideas and practices, but also artistic techniques. Above all, they introduced learning and literature into Japan, first by spreading among the aristocracy a knowledge of the Chinese language, and then, in the eighth and ninth centuries, by helping to create a Japanese script out of Chinese ideographs.

This adaptation of a Chinese technique to Japan's own requirements showed that Japan did not intend to become a mere imitation of a Chinese province. Chinese might remain the language of learning and greater prestige, but creative Japanese were turning towards their own tongue as the medium of literary expression. Among the Japanese writers of the Heian period (794–1185) the most outstanding was a court lady, Murasaki Shikibu, whose long novel of aristocratic life, *The Tale of Genji*, holds a recognised place in world literature. She and other court ladies gave Heian culture much of its unique delicacy and sensitivity.

The bureaucratic system of government inspired by China had little chance of long-term success because it depended on the sense of public duty of aristocratic officials who were under constant temptation to feather their own nests at the state's expense. Indeed, the government would probably have lost its authority by the tenth century had it not been supported by the Fujiwara family. From the mid-ninth century successive heads of this great house held the position of regent, even when the emperor was an adult. By constantly marrying their daughters into the imperial family, moreover, they were able to dominate every emperor. Only in the mid-eleventh century did their marriage policy fail, and by then their influence had been weakened by a more general shift of power.

The weakening of state control over the provinces forced local land-

10

owners to form armed bands or seek protection from military chieftains. Gradually well-organised provincial forces appeared and a new type of professional warrior, knowing no loyalty other than that which he owed to his leader. This was the genesis of the *samurai* (or *bushi*) class, which would dominate Japan for many centuries.

By the mid-twelfth century, two outstanding military leagues had emerged. By an ironic twist of history, both the Taira, who were at first in the ascendant, and the Minamoto, who eventually triumphed under the leadership of Yoritomo, were the descendants of ninth-century emperors. Their lineage gave them prestige among their followers and helped Yoritomo to reach a compromise with the court. He received imperial appointment as *shōgun* (commander-in-chief) in 1192, but retained an independent headquarters (*bakufu*) at Kamakura, near modern Tōkyō.

The Kamakura *bakufu* at first co-existed with the old civil government, but gradually it encroached more and more on its functions until by the fifteenth century the imperial court was powerless and impoverished. The feudal régime soon encountered serious problems itself, however, the most notable being the Mongol invasions of 1274 and 1281. These were the only military expeditions against Japan recorded before the nineteenth century, but they represented a very real danger, backed as they were by the resources of China, which Khublai Khan had just subjugated. On both occasions, Japanese determination and valour proved sufficient to hold their lines of defence until the enemy armadas were threatened with destruction by typhoons—gratefully termed by the Japanese *kamikaze* (divine wind).

Eventually a number of regional lords, headed by Ashikaga Takauji, overthrew the Kamakura *bakufu* in 1333. But the Ashikaga shogunate which replaced it proved to be even weaker, though it survived in name till 1573. Except for a partial pause in the early fifteenth century, constant warfare was the rule in almost every province during the Ashikaga period. So intense did it become that the hundred years following the Ōnin War (1467–77) are known as the *Sengoku jidai* (period of warring provinces).

At the height of the *Sengoku jidai*, in 1543, some Portuguese sailors were blown off course in the China Sea and became the first Europeans to visit Japan. They were followed by other Portuguese, both traders and missionaries, and the efforts of the latter led to the conversion of large numbers of Japanese, perhaps half a million in all, to Catholicism. Eventually, in the 1630s, all the Portuguese were expelled, and the only foreigners permitted

The Hōryūji, a great temple in Japan's first permanent capital city of Nara.
Established with the help of Prince Shōtoku Taishi in 607, it is believed to be the oldest
surviving wooden building in the world

to visit Japan were a few Dutch and Chinese traders. Already by the 1560s,
however, the Portuguese musket had been imitated and was revolutionising
warfare in Japan. Instead of largely individual fighting between mounted
samurai armed with swords and bows, massed formations of riflemen could
now be employed with devastating effect. First to appreciate the new
possibilities were Oda Nobunaga, son of a petty *daimyō* (feudal lord), and
his general, Toyotomi Hideyoshi.

Nobunaga was betrayed and assassinated in 1582, when he had gained
control of central Japan. His death was swiftly revenged by Hideyoshi,
who then proceeded in a series of rapid campaigns to subdue those *daimyō*
who refused to acknowledge his supremacy. By 1590 he was able to turn
his attention to Japan's neighbours, and in 1592 he launched a military
expedition which swiftly over-ran Korea. Before it could cross into China,
however, the Ming dynasty, appreciating the danger, sent troops to Korea

itself. Warfare continued for several years until the stalemate was ended by Hideyoshi's death in 1598 and Japanese withdrawal. It is worth noting that this was the only occasion on which a Japanese ruler had encroached upon another state since the seventh century.

Hideyoshi's death was followed by another struggle for power in Japan. Out of it emerged a ruler whose position was stronger than that of any of his predecessors. Following his victory at Sekigahara in 1600, Tokugawa Ieyasu, once a minor *daimyō* and ally of Nobunaga, increased his own domains far beyond those of his *daimyō* rivals. His establishment of a new shogunate in 1603 marked the beginning of the Tokugawa period, during which Japan enjoyed two and a half centuries of peace. It was still in existence when the Western Powers determined to re-open Japan after two hundred years of exclusion.

This historical background helps to explain Japan's distinctive response to the nineteenth-century Western challenge in three main ways. In the first place there existed a tradition of borrowing from abroad. From at least the time of the Taika Reform Japan had looked to China for cultural inspiration. Moreover, by the late eighteenth century Japanese scholars who had gained a rudimentary knowledge of the West by learning Dutch had understood that in material and scientific matters Europe had advanced beyond the East. Japan was therefore prepared to accept Western methods and models to an extent quite impossible for China, which retained a much deeper conviction of its own superiority.

The second important legacy was rule by a military class. Far more than the mandarins who governed China, the *samurai* were conscious of the importance of military technology. It was their concern with this aspect of European superiority which chiefly explains the emergence of Japan by the end of the century as a power able to defend itself by arms.

Such a resolution on the part of the ruling class might have been far less effective, however, had it not been for the third major historical factor—Japan's deep-rooted nationalism. Traditions of racial and political unity were reinforced by a deep awareness of separate cultural identity, largely the product of Japan's geographical isolation. Although Japan had borrowed much from China she had adapted it to evolve a distinctive and independent style of her own. It was because she was the least orthodox of the societies dominated by Chinese culture that Japan was also the most untypical in her response to the nineteenth-century challenge.

2

Traditional Society

Japan in 1850 was quite unlike any other society. Culturally she still bore traces of the earlier Chinese imprint, but politically she had almost nothing in common with her neighbours. From European countries she stood even further apart. Her most unique feature was her extraordinary stability. Even the size of her population had remained almost constant at roughly 26–30 millions from the 1720s until the mid-nineteenth century. This contrasted strikingly with what was happening at the same time in almost every other part of the world. In part the population control was the result of famines caused by a succession of bad harvests in the 1730s, 1780s and 1830s. There was also, however, an element of conscious limitation, mainly in the shape of infanticide (*mabiki*, meaning literally 'thinning the crop'). It foreshadowed another successful attempt to control population growth in the early 1950s, though this time the main instrument used was abortion.

Infanticide was officially frowned upon, but in all other respects the central government, the Tokugawa *bakufu*, did its utmost to encourage stability. The *bakufu* was the administrative headquarters established by Ieyasu, and in theory it should have served Ieyasu's fourteen successors as it had him, but by the eighteenth century it was rare to find a *shōgun* willing or able to give up the easy pleasures of the shogunal court for the

Himeji Castle, built at the beginning of the Tokugawa period, is generally regarded as the most impressive surviving example of the period of intensive castle-building in Japan

time-consuming work of government. Decision-making passed into the hands of Tokugawa officials, generally *fudai daimyō* (hereditary Tokugawa retainers), who tended to regard themselves as stewards entrusted with the maintenance of established policy.

The essence of that policy was the outlawing of change, and the success of the *bakufu* was shown by the total peace which Japan enjoyed for over two hundred years. This remarkable achievement was founded on a division of land which placed more than two-thirds of the country, including the strategically important central belt between Edo and Kyōto, under the direct control of the Tokugawa family or its feudal allies and retainers. The *bakufu* could live off its own without needing to impose regular taxes on the feudal lords, the *daimyō*. The *daimyō* were not completely independent of the central power, however, for they were all compelled to spend alternate years (*sankin-kōtai*) in the Tokugawa capital of Edo—now Tōkyō. Even when they were able to return home to their domains (*han*) they had to leave their wives and children behind as hostages. In addition, the *bakufu* ensured that its potential enemies did not plot together by separating the domains of the *tozama daimyō* (outside lords) and by sending spies into their territories.

As a final precautionary measure, the Tokugawa *bakufu* determined to prevent any hostile *daimyō* from seeking foreign assistance by severing Japan's connections with the outside world in the 1630s. No Japanese was permitted to leave the country or build ocean-going ships, and the handful of Chinese and Dutch traders who were allowed into the country were kept under strict surveillance in the Tokugawa port of Nagasaki. By this *sakoku* (closed country) policy the *bakufu* consolidated Japan's political stability and removed the short-term threat of a foreign religion, but at the long-term cost of greatly widening the technological gap between Europe and Japan.

Ingenious and thorough as the Tokugawa system of control was, it could hardly have survived unchanged if it had not been supported by other measures closely regulating Japanese society. One way of ensuring stability was to reduce social mobility to a minimum by rigidly separating the various classes of society and forbidding movement between them. At the top came the *samurai* class which alone had the right to bear weapons. Its members enjoyed the privilege of *kirisute-gomen*—the right to cut down with one of their two deadly swords any non-*samurai* who insulted them. This was a legacy of earlier centuries, when many *samurai* had possessed their own fiefs. They had good cause to be proud of their status and had developed their own code of behaviour, known as *bushidō* (the way of the warrior).

Bushidō bore some resemblance to European chivalry. It was narrower in that it had no religious overtones (although many *samurai* found meaning in Zen Buddhism), did not idealise women or love, and confined itself to relations between *samurai*. It was more far reaching, however, in that it placed an even greater emphasis on loyalty. No *samurai* could have more than one lord and the relationship between the two was more one-sided than in European feudalism. A *samurai* was expected to die for his lord if necessary, and there could be no question of surrender if defeated in battle. Rather than lose his honour the *samurai* was expected to commit *seppuku* or *hara-kiri*, the ritual sacrifice of one's life by cutting deeply into and across one's stomach, with a fellow *samurai* shortening one's agony by slicing off one's head with a single stroke of his sword.

Though the *samurai* were still essentially concerned with the arts of war in 1600, by the nineteenth century the permanent peace had converted many of them into administrators rather than warriors. They were very numerous for a ruling class—about six per cent of the population—and within their ranks were numerous subdivisions ranging from the *daimyō* to the *ashigaru*, or foot-soldier, who was often economically worse off than a good many commoners. It was status which mattered most, however, in Tokugawa Japan, in theory at least. By that criterion every *samurai*, however poor, enjoyed a hereditary superiority over all the members of the three other main classes.

Of those other classes, the most numerous by far was the peasantry. They formed more than eighty per cent of the population and it was they who shouldered the main burden of supporting the state by taxation. Scattered all over Honshū, Kyūshū, and Shikoku in some 70,000 villages, which themselves generally included several separate hamlets, the peasants were far too divided to challenge the supremacy of the *samurai*, even if they had not been grateful for the Tokugawa peace, which guaranteed that some portion, at least, of their crops—usually between one-half and two-thirds—would remain in their hands and not be seized by *samurai* armies or brigands. Peasant rebellion was made especially difficult by the 'Sword Hunt' carried out in 1588 by Hideyoshi, whereby sword-bearing villagers had to choose whether they should give up their land and claim *samurai* status or remain in the village as unarmed peasants. One result was that later revolts were always confined to demands for the redress of specific grievances, and never attempted to overthrow authority.

The basic factor governing the lives of the peasantry was Japan's climate. High levels of rainfall and sunshine permitted rice cultivation everywhere south of Hokkaidō, and the nature of rice cultivation goes a long way towards explaining the stability of Tokugawa society. More than in Western feudal society the Japanese peasant was tied to the soil. By the eighteenth century all the easily cultivable land had been made into paddy, and to leave an existing holding and create a new one was an enormously laborious undertaking. A hillside plot would have had to be cleared of vegetation and levelled, and the soil would have had to be specially layered to a depth of three feet to provide the right drainage for the rice plants. Above all, a supply of water would have had to be laid on by some form of irrigation, and this was beyond the capability of any single family. Thus no peasant could leave his land without abandoning both his status and his security.

The other way in which rice cultivation encouraged stability lay in its high productivity. Most family holdings were less than one and a quarter acres, yet even so agriculture produced enough to support a ruling class far larger than those of Europe. So secure did this make the *bakufu* and *daimyō* feel, indeed, that they almost all regarded their *samurai* retainers as a greater potential danger than the peasantry and brought them into their castle-towns where they could keep them under close control. As long as the land tax was paid, the villagers were left to themselves, with governmental authority being delegated to the village headman.

This rigid separation of political power from direct ownership of land was one of the most unusual features of Tokugawa society. It was to be extremely significant for Japanese modernisation since it prevented the formation of a conservative, landowning, ruling class, which might have been opposed to industrialisation. However, this did not mean that a landlord class did not emerge to a limited extent within the villages. It is estimated that by 1850 about twenty per cent of the land had come under tenancy, and some of the new landlords were able to use their wealth to set up commercial enterprises such as brewing *sake*, the Japanese rice wine.

Despite the growth of inequality, the hamlet remained a tightly knit community, where the traditional desire for harmony softened the effects of economic differences. Undoubtedly the family relationship which existed between many landlords and tenants played a part in this, but there was also an economic need for harmony. The intensive labour requirements at the time of transplanting and harvesting made co-operation essential, and so did the necessity of finding a fair solution to the problem of water-sharing. This was so vital that suspicion and conflict could easily have arisen and disrupted the whole village.

Similarly, co-operation was necessary to maintain the irrigation network and the paths which gave families access to their separate plots of land. These, and a host of other communal tasks and undertakings, were carried out by representatives of each household. So important was village solidarity considered, indeed, that it was not unknown for village assemblies to meet informally to settle differences of opinion in advance, so that their formal gatherings might not be marred by any disagreement. This sort of attitude goes a long way towards explaining the high degree of formal politeness in Japanese society. Since, in addition, every household belonged to a neighbourhood group which was held collectively responsible if one member committed a crime, it is easy to understand why there was no place for individualism in the Japanese village.

Scene from a painted screen of the sixteenth century showing Japanese peasants at work in the fields

Despite this powerful tendency towards social conformity, however, sufficient initiative was shown by enough farmers in the development and propagation of new crops, improved strains of rice and agricultural implements to raise productivity considerably between the seventeenth and nineteenth centuries. Since much of this new wealth went unnoticed by the feudal rulers in their castle-towns, the result was a distinct improvement in the standard of living of at least some peasants. A surprising number were able to buy books and pay for their children to be educated. There were 10,000 or so small local schools in Japan known as *terakoya*, mostly run by private teachers, although earlier Buddhist temples had played the leading part in instructing commoners. By 1850 forty per cent of the total male population could read and write and more than ten per cent of the female, figures which compare favourably with many European countries at that time.

The well-being of the peasantry should not be exaggerated. Some were too poor to eat the rice they grew except on festive days. Meat and milk were virtually unknown, and, except on the coast, fish was tasted only rarely. Millet and barley were the normal food for many, with pickled vegetables providing flavour and soya-beans most of the protein. Nevertheless, the average Japanese was undoubtedly better off than his counterpart in other countries of Asia at that time.

Compared with the *samurai* and the peasantry the artisans and merchants were both newcomers as major classes. Both had expanded rapidly during the seventeenth century when the coming of the Tokugawa peace and the establishment of the *sankin-kōtai* (alternate attendance) system brought the *daimyō* into Edo and led to rapid urban growth. Edo itself was transformed in this period, expanding from a small castle-town into a great capital. With a population of perhaps one million in 1700, it ranked as one of the major cities of the world. Osaka, the commercial centre of Japan, contained just under half this number, but was almost as wealthy and as a seat of culture certainly not inferior. The artisans, who were mainly craftsmen practising traditional skills, such as lacquer-work or the making of *tatami* (straw mats), profited less from this development than the merchants, who were able to take advantage of *samurai* disdain for commercial and financial dealings. It was the merchants who took over the lucrative business of selling the rice which the *daimyō* had to market in order to pay the many expenses incurred in travelling to Edo and living there. Eventually merchants also became money-lenders to *daimyō* and in this way sometimes amassed enormous fortunes. Their wealth, however, was not a true reflection of their position in society, and although they might be treated with deference by needy *daimyō*, ultimately they had no political power. Nevertheless, they made an enduring contribution to Japanese civilisation by their support of new developments in popular culture.

The four main classes did not constitute the whole of Japanese society. They did not include priests and monks, for example. Although Christianity was suppressed in the seventeenth century, Japan still had two major religions, Buddhism and Shintō. Most Japanese found nothing incongruous in belonging to one of the many varieties of Buddhism and at the same time worshipping at the local Shintō shrine. The two religions had generally existed side by side without difficulty, and in many places the Shintō shrine

20

So little of Japan's land surface is suitable for cultivation ▶
that many hills have had to be painstakingly terraced

was actually tended by a Buddhist priest. They complemented, rather than competed with, each other.

Buddhism had originally been an essentially aristocratic creed, but from the thirteenth century it became spiritually important for most Japanese. The two Pure Land sects, in particular, won many followers by preaching that the Pure Land (*nirvana*, paradise) could be attained by the invocation of Buddha's name. In their directness and simplicity and in allowing priests to marry, they bore some resemblance to Protestantism.

Shintō (the Way of the Gods) was the native religion of Japan. It had no real theology, yet it remained fundamental in the lives of ordinary Japanese for it reflected their deepest feelings about nature and human society. On the one hand Shintō expressed reverence towards exceptional phenomena, whether they were powerful destructive forces such as typhoons, objects of outstanding natural beauty such as Mount Fuji, or mythological heroes. All were regarded as *kami* (superior), possessors of special power. Side by side with this reverence went a fertility cult, involving rituals mostly connected with rice, and a dread of impurity, one manifestation of which continues today in the form of the daily family bath. On the other hand, Shintō was connected with the Japanese ideal of village solidarity in that the local shrine provided a unifying focal point for the village. There were, however, some shrines in the Yamato area which had a national importance and were visited by an increasing number of pilgrims, for most of whom it would be the nearest thing to a holiday they would ever experience.

On its social side, Shintō derived much of its support from Confucianism, the basic moral philosophy of China, which had long been known in Japan, but became particularly significant in the Tokugawa period. Confucianism offered a guide to harmonious conduct which corresponded closely with Japanese feeling for hierarchy and hereditary status. On the one hand it emphasised the unequal nature of human society by stressing the superiority of rulers over subjects, fathers over sons, husbands over wives, and elder brothers over younger brothers. On the other hand, Confucianism inculcated the idea that everyone was born into their rightful place in society and should perform as well as possible the duties associated with that place without seeking to change it. Confucian teaching was strongly encouraged by the *bakufu* and *daimyō* because it generally treated rulers as uniquely fitted to govern by their possession of wisdom and virtue. It was particularly important for the *samurai* class, for it provided an ethical backing for the demand of absolute loyalty which the feudal lord made on his vassals but which he could no longer expect as warrior-leader. Confucian scholars were employed by all *daimyō* in the *han* schools which were established for *samurai* youths in the Tokugawa period and their influence has not completely disappeared even today.

Where Confucianism and Shintō combined most effectively was in helping to shape the Japanese family system. Both emphasised reverence towards family ancestors and the duty of obedience to the family head. The family was magnified as the basic unit of society and the wishes of its individual members were subordinated to the household as a whole. Marriages, for example, were frequently arranged by family-heads, working through go-betweens and considering family interests as much as the personal wishes of the bride and bridegroom-to-be. This custom was not yet practised widely among the peasantry, who followed a variety of local traditions, some of which were extremely permissive. Even in the villages, however, it was not uncommon for a daughter-in-law to be divorced for not gaining the family's approval, even though she might be personally pleasing to her husband.

The authority of the family-head was reflected in the privileges given to the elder son, who was treated with deference by any sisters and younger brothers because it was he who would succeed to the headship of the family and take over custody of the family property. If a family failed to produce a son, it would almost invariably adopt one to prevent the extinction of the family line. Sometimes it might be necessary to adopt someone who had already reached manhood, a step which inevitably posed personal problems but was accepted for the family's sake. It goes almost without saying that the status of women was inferior, though peasant women probably enjoyed considerable influence in practice, because their labour in the fields was as important as that of the men.

The extent to which adoption occurred made the Japanese family unusual, but what really sets the Japanese family-system apart from practices anywhere else is its use as a model for other social organisations. It would seem that the Japanese have been so impressed by the strength and cohesiveness of the family that many other relationships are thought of in family terms. *Samurai* were often regarded as their *daimyō*'s *ie no ko* (child of the household), and, at a higher level, the Tokugawa family sometimes bestowed upon *daimyō* its own original name of Matsudaira. A similar pseudo-kinship pattern was also widespread among artisans and

23

This print by Utamaro (1753–1806) of an artist painting a landscape evokes the feminine grace and the more easy-going relationships between men and women in certain urban areas in Tokugawa Japan

craftsmen, who would treat an outstanding pupil as a son and pass on to him their skills and name if they had no gifted son of their own.

Far from disappearing when Japan began to modernise, this practice of establishing *oyabun-kobun* (parent role–child role) relationships spread into new fields. It even infiltrated Japanese politics, where political factions, organised on a basis of personal loyalty towards the leader and modelled on the *daimyō-samurai* relationship, have generally been more important than either parties or principles. Its influence can be greater than that of legal authority. The chief statesmen of the Meiji era (1868–1912), for instance, were able to dominate politics even after their own retirement because their wishes were deferred to by the men they had sponsored and placed in high office. Professors have been known to suppress their own opinions because they conflicted with those of the teachers who had been their patrons. Such hidden ties are probably the largest cause of confusion to the foreigner seeking to understand Japan.

No account of traditional Japanese society would be complete without some reference to the imperial house. Although by this time the emperors had long lost their ruling power, the imperial institution retained too much prestige and sanctity to be abolished by Japan's military leaders, even if they had been so inclined. In fact, it was useful to the *shōgun* because it could be induced to sanction and legitimise the Tokugawa seizure of power. In return for imperial acknowledgement of the *shōgun*'s right to govern, the *bakufu* relieved the court from the poverty which it had suffered in the fifteenth and sixteenth centuries as a result of the erosion of its income from taxes and estates. No serious Japanese foresaw in 1850 that in less than twenty years the whole Tokugawa system would be overthrown and the imperial prerogatives revived.

Tokugawa society was not quite as static, however, as the apparent permanence of the political system made it seem. Economic development had taken place and was continuing, though it was tending to shift from the now-conservative merchants in the towns to the rising class of landlords with industrial or commercial interests in the countryside. Education was being extended to an ever larger number of people, and knowledge of the West was being increasingly acquired and disseminated by the growing band of scholars who had with great difficulty learned Dutch in order to read the books which could be obtained through the traders at Nagasaki. Culturally, too, it was a period of great vitality. *Kabuki*, a colourful musical melodrama, in which female parts are played exclusively by male actors, and *Bunraku*, a sophisticated and stylised form of puppet theatre, were developed, while the Japanese land and people were vividly portrayed by Hokusai, Hiroshige, and many other masters of the new, cheap colour-print, and by such popular novelists and poets as Saikaku and Bashō. Even socially there was a growing tendency for merchants to acquire *samurai* rank through marriage or adoption and for village headmen to assert themselves as the equals of *samurai*. All these developments gave hints that Japan was capable of change.

3

The End
of Isolation

In July 1853 four black American warships sailed into Tōkyō Bay. Their
commander, Commodore Matthew C. Perry, was to become famous as the
man who ended Japanese isolation. Yet this was far from being the first
attempt to open Japan. By the mid-nineteenth century Japan had already
been successfully resisting such efforts for over fifty years. Promises, threats
and even the occasional display of force had all served to strengthen
Japan's resolve to keep herself separate. Why, then, did Japan agree to
negotiate at last?

The basic difference in 1853 was that British military success against
China had opened a new era in Japanese thinking. Grossly exaggerated
reports of the Opium War (1839–42) had quickly circulated in Japan,
hard on the heels of a rumour of a British fleet of 25,000 ships. It was clear
that in the face of such massive power the old policy of outright refusal to
negotiate was highly dangerous. How, then, was Japan to maintain her
independence and, if possible, her seclusion? The problem was still
unresolved when Perry appeared, with a larger force than had previously
been seen in Japanese waters and the firm intention of not returning home
empty-handed.

The *bakufu*'s reluctance to admit foreigners to Japan was not due solely
to prejudice. It was also related to the changed nature of Tokugawa
power. Two centuries of peace had eroded Tokugawa military strength,

but as long as the traditional system remained unchanged no *daimyō* would think of endangering the peace which the Tokugawa system of government guaranteed. Once the security and stability of Japan were threatened, however, Tokugawa rule would come into question.

Desire to maintain traditional policy, therefore, was tremendously strong within the *bakufu*. Should war occur, however, the *bakufu* would bear the brunt of the fighting. Edo, the Tokugawa capital, might be blockaded, or even bombarded. The *bakufu* stood to lose heavily, therefore, both if it rejected the American demands and if it abandoned seclusion. In the face of its dilemma it bought time by promising a reply to Perry's requests when he returned to Japan the following year.

It was fortunate for the *bakufu* that its senior council was presided over at this time by a *fudai daimyō* of considerable political insight—thirty-four-year-old Abe Masahiro. Instead of confining foreign policy decisions to *bakufu* officials alone, Abe took the unprecedented step of seeking the opinions of the semi-independent *tozama daimyō*. Only a few were inclined to accept Perry's demands, but at the same time those who were prepared to risk war were a minority. This division of opinion gave Abe room for manoeuvre, and soon after Perry returned, with eight ships, in February 1854, he yielded on the less essential points. In March a treaty was signed with America at Kanagawa providing for the good treatment of ship-wrecked sailors, the appointment of consuls, and the opening, for supplies only, of two unimportant ports, Shimoda and Hakodate. The *bakufu* could still claim that there had been no basic change in traditional policy, and neither the *daimyō* nor the imperial court protested.

Against the odds, Abe had succeeded in satisfying everyone. His compromise policy of consulting the most able *tozama daimyō* and promoting men of ability soon encountered opposition, however, among the *fudai daimyō*—the hundred or so descendants of Ieyasu's retainers who monopolised the chief *bakufu* offices. The immediate crisis having passed, they argued that Japan's stability and independence could only be maintained by a strict continuation of the traditional system. In November 1855 Abe resigned as chief minister rather than be completely excluded later. His successor, Hotta Masayoshi, was the man of his choice, but much of Abe's compromise approach towards other *daimyō* was lost. By turning back to tradition the *bakufu* was taking a step towards its own destruction.

In 1858 the *bakufu* was faced with a new and much graver crisis than that of 1853. In the previous year the Arrow War had again brought

Commodore Perry's officers encountering Japanese *sumo* wrestlers. Already a traditional sport in the nineteenth century, *sumo* today enjoys immense popularity, mainly through television

British and French naval power to bear on China. Townsend Harris, the American consul in Shimoda, saw the chance of furthering his own fruitless negotiations for an improved treaty by exaggerating the threat to Japan. He argued that if a new Japanese–American treaty had not been signed before the British and French arrived, they would impose a much more one-sided one on Japan. This reasoning eventually convinced Hotta. Rather than be opened by force, it would be better for Japan to accept a controlled relationship with Western nations and learn their techniques. By late February 1858 a new treaty was ready to be signed.

At this point the *bakufu* ran into difficulties. The new treaty went much further than the previous one. It opened for trade, either immediately or within five years, the important ports and cities of Nagasaki, Kanagawa (Yokohama), Niigata, Hyōgo (Kōbe), Edo, and Ōsaka, and allowed the establishment of a diplomatic legation in Edo. When the details were made known, there were serious rumblings of discontent among the *daimyō* and to offset their criticism Hotta decided to secure the approval of the imperial court for the treaty. He little suspected that by so doing he would precipitate his own downfall and create untold problems for the shogunate.

Many centuries had passed since an emperor had exercised any real political power. What part he would play now, therefore, was not easy to forecast. Most of the senior court officials favoured a policy of caution, but many lesser court nobles, encouraged by *samurai* from the great *han*, who shared the former's resentment at their exclusion from governmental power, saw in the crisis an opportunity to revive the old prestige of the throne by increasing *bakufu* embarrassment. As a result of their scheming a decree was issued ordering the *bakufu* to maintain the seclusion policy. Hotta returned to Edo convinced that if the *bakufu* was to settle the foreign question it would have to calm the court by making some concessions to the *daimyō* who had been responsible for arousing imperial pretensions.

Hotta failed to reckon with the intrenched conservatism of the *fudai daimyō*. They had not seen the growing strength of opposition to their hereditary monopoly of power. Their reaction took the form of a return to Tokugawa authoritarianism. Ii Naosuke, *daimyō* of the largest *fudai han* was appointed shogunal regent. He then removed from office Hotta and other moderate supporters of the recently deceased Abe and on 29 July 1858 the new American treaty was signed without imperial approval.

The most extreme action was yet to come, however. On 13 August Ii set in motion a purge of *bakufu* opponents and critics. Despite their status, many of the most important *daimyō* were confined to their residences or forced to retire, and their most active retainers were arrested and executed. Some nobles were even punished by being compelled to become priests.

By the end of 1858 the *bakufu* appeared to have surmounted its crisis. The American treaty had been followed by similar ones with Holland, Russia, Britain and France. Within Japan, the opponents of the *bakufu* had been silenced. By his harsh actions, however, Ii Naosuke had thrown away much valuable goodwill. Resentful *samurai* were already beginning to take up and link together the slogans *sonnō* (revere the Emperor) and *jōi* (expel the barbarian). With foreign traders due to arrive in 1859, Japan was not likely to remain calm for long.

4

The Samurai
Revolution

More than any other single action Ii Naosuke's attempt to revive authoritarian Tokugawa rule sealed the fate of the shogunate. Before the 1850s politics on a national scale did not exist in Japan. After 1858 the harmony which had safeguarded the Tokugawa *status quo* was at an end. In the next ten years Japan would resemble Pandora's box opened as all the latent antagonisms and frustrations came to the surface.

These deeper sources of unrest were to prove far more dangerous for the shogunate than *daimyō* jealousies. The most important, attested to by the prevalence and emotive force of the slogan *jōi*, was the sense of foreign threat. Unleashing, as it did, the latent forces of nationalism, it played a crucial role in bringing about radical change in Japan. Nevertheless, the speed with which *samurai* leaders who had called for the expulsion of foreigners adjusted to their continued presence once they were themselves in power does suggest that *jōi* served as a cloak for other motives also.

Chief among these other motives was *samurai* discontent. Almost all *samurai* resented merchant prosperity, and many of them suffered more directly when indebted *daimyō* cut their stipends. The major *samurai* grievance, however, was inequality of opportunity. Lower *samurai* who had excelled in the *han* schools saw less talented *samurai* of higher rank filling the more influential positions. It was their aspirations, unspoken at first and perhaps unconscious, which created the internal drive for a less rigid social system. In most of the active *han* they received support from village headmen who resented *han* attempts to encroach upon their commercial activities. Nevertheless, in terms of leadership the Meiji Restoration—the replacement of the *bakufu* by an imperial government in 1868—was to be essentially a *samurai* revolution.

In March 1860 Ii Naosuke paid the price for his dictatorial action. In the snow outside Edo castle he was assassinated by *samurai* seeking vengeance. His death shook *bakufu* confidence and prompted a revival of Abe's compromise policy under the name of *kōbu-gattai* (union of court and military).

Until 1864 it appeared that this attempt at conservative reform had a real chance of success. At the urging of Shimazu Hisamitsu, lord of the powerful Satsuma *han*, the *bakufu* agreed to major reforms, including appointment of the reformist Hitotsubashi Keiki as guardian of the *shōgun*. Meanwhile, however, *sonnō-jōi samurai* flocked to Kyōto and pressurised the court into demanding the immediate expulsion of foreigners. The *bakufu* dared not retaliate and had to pretend to comply with the court's wish. In September 1863, however, Satsuma forces expelled them from Kyōto and freed the court from *samurai* control.

The fact that Satsuma had done what the *bakufu* had not dared to do was a grave blow to the shogunate's prestige. Even Hitotsubashi Keiki came to resent Satsuma influence. In March 1864 the uneasy coalition split when Hisamitsu offered to persuade the court to revoke its expulsion order. Because so open a reversal of nominally accepted policy would further increase Satsuma's standing, Keiki opposed it, and the breach was sealed when he subjected Hisamitsu to a torrent of drunken insults.

One of the reasons why the *bakufu* dared to alienate Satsuma was that by this time it felt less threatened from outside. This marked a striking change from the situation immediately following the opening of the ports in 1859. At that time foreign relations had been fraught with tension and difficulties. Attacks by loyalist *samurai*, enraged at what they considered a violation of Japanese soil, were a constant hazard to foreigners. The Western ministers suspected the *shōgun*'s officials of taking insufficient precautions to prevent such unofficial attempts to drive them from Japan and were constantly writing home to ask for stronger naval backing.

In time, however, foreign diplomats came to recognise that the *bakufu*, having already incurred the charge of national betrayal by opening Japan, dared not risk further unpopularity by suppressing anti-foreign activities.

31

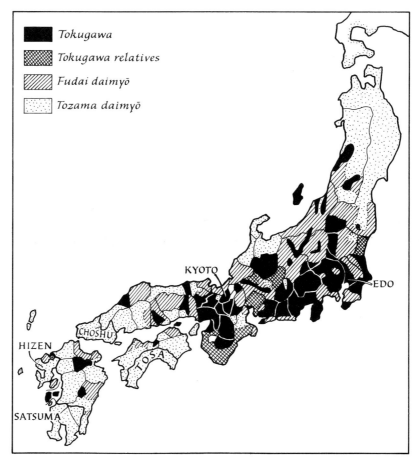

THE FEUDAL DIVISIONS OF TOKUGAWA JAPAN

With this recognition came a realisation that new tactics were required. In August 1863 a British naval force was sent to bombard Kagoshima, the capital of Satsuma, in retaliation for the murder of an English merchant named Richardson. The following year, the British minister, Alcock, organised an allied expedition of seventeen ships against the stronghold of the imperial loyalists, Chōsū. Its successful assault on the port of Shimonoseki was a telling demonstration of Western military power and it ended the campaign to expel foreigners.

The Shimonoseki expedition proved a turning-point also in the *bakufu*'s relations with the Western powers. Whereas Alcock was replaced by Sir Harry Parkes, a believer in 'gunboat diplomacy' as a means of ensuring that oriental governments respected Western rights, France was now represented by Léon Roches, who respected Japanese qualities and abilities and, in accordance with his ambition of fathering Japan's modernisation, did his utmost to strengthen the shogunate. Although the French government agreed, however, to requests from the *bakufu* and Roches to send military advisers, as well as engineers who began to construct a large dockyard at Yokosuka, it did not share Roches' deep commitment to the Tokugawa shogunate, and the material advantages of this special relationship with France were in the end outweighed by political disadvantages.

Already by 1865 the failure of *kōbu-gattai* had weakened Hisamitsu's position in Satsuma, and influence was shifting towards Saigō Takamori and Ōkubo Toshimichi, *samurai* leaders who had close ties with the loyalists. With fear of a *bakufu*–French alliance as a spur and with Sakamoto Ryōma, a Tosa *samurai*, acting as go-between, the bitter rivalry between Satsuma and Chōshū was smoothed over, and a secret alliance signed pledging both *han* to the destruction of the *bakufu*.

In 1866 *bakufu* forces attacked Chōshū and suffered a dismal defeat. Keiki, now *shōgun*, realised at last that real sacrifices of authority must be made by the *bakufu*. In November 1867 he grasped at the Tosa *daimyō*'s suggestion that he should hand back the *shōgun*'s powers voluntarily to the Emperor and accept a *daimyō* council over which he himself would preside. At first the plan seemed to have worked. On 3 January 1868, however, Saigō Takamori seized the imperial palace in Kyōto, and proclaimed the full restoration of power to the Emperor, a youth known generally by his reign-name of Meiji (Shining Government).

In the civil war which followed, the coalition which centred on the south-western *han* of Satsuma and Chōshū had several important advantages. It controlled the Emperor, it had troops of proven worth, and it enjoyed the cautious sympathy of the British minister, Sir Harry Parkes. Above all, the Tokugawa leaders were deeply disunited. Some *fudai daimyō* wanted to oppose the south-western *han* to the bitter end, but Keiki knew that Tokugawa authority could never be restored. Rather than subject the country to a bitter civil war he finally decided to accept the imperial confiscation of most of the shogunal domain. Edo was surrendered in May, and, although some northern *han* resisted the south-western forces fiercely, the real issue was already settled.

The Tokugawa surrender did not mean that the political problems of the new government were over. On the contrary, there were to follow five years of intricate manoeuvring before anything like stability was achieved.

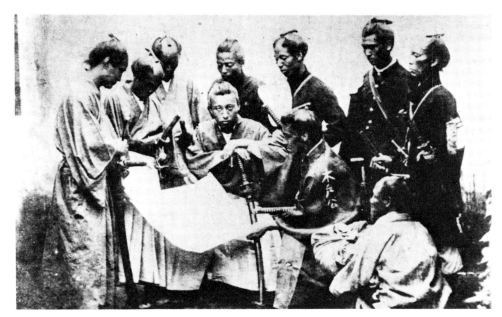

Some of the *samurai* who brought about the overthrow of the Tokugawa *bakufu*. Seated second from the right is Kido Kōin (Chōshū); on his right, leaning on his sword, may be Sakamoto Ryōma (Tosa) who was murdered in late 1867; and second from the right is Itō Hirobumi (Chōshū), later one of the chief architects of Japanese modernisation.

Foreign intervention, counter-revolution and anarchy were all on the cards in 1868. They were only avoided by the exceptional skill of certain *samurai* reformers.

These *samurai* reformers were surprisingly few in number. Their main leaders were Saigō and Ōkubo from Satsuma and Kido from Chōshū. Their *samurai* status varied, though most had originally been middle- or low-ranking, and they were fairly young—in their thirties in most cases. All shared a determination to change and strengthen Japan. Unlike many of their fellow *samurai*, they had thrown off their *jōi* blinkers and understood that it was necessary to learn from the West if their country was not to be taken over by the West.

The obstacles these reformers faced were huge. The coalition they had organised represented various divergent interests. Apart from the in-experienced young Emperor, it included reactionary court nobles who hoped for a return to Japan's distant imperial past, and conservative *daimyō* who wished to retain feudal institutions. Because of their rank, moreover, these groups held most of the high offices in the new government.

34

Nevertheless, the *samurai* reformers eventually emerged triumphant. By 1873 it was they who were monopolising the government and their policies which were being implemented. They had been fortunate in having as allies two court nobles, Iwakura Tomomi and Sanjō Sanetomi, and it was also possible for them to play court nobles and *daimyō* off against each other. Their greatest advantage, however, was that they were the only ones with a real solution to Japan's problems.

The steps by which the *samurai* reformers advanced their own power were also landmarks in Japan's political modernisation. May 1869 saw the transfer of the Emperor's residence to Edo, now renamed Tōkyō (Eastern Capital). Two months earlier an even more significant change had been set in motion when the *daimyō* of Satsuma, Chōshū, Tosa and Hizen were persuaded to offer their *han* to the Emperor. In July all *daimyō* were enjoined to do likewise. Though it seemed only a symbolic gesture, since the *daimyō* continued to rule their domains in the Emperor's name, it paved the way for the complete abolition of feudal institutions.

Even a series of minor *samurai* rebellions did not deter Ōkubo and his colleagues from pursuing their aims. In 1870 approaches were made to France for a military mission to train the nucleus of a modern army, and a one million pound loan was floated in London to finance the building of Japan's first railway, from Tōkyō to Yokohama. In the following year, the formation of the new imperial army from Satsuma, Chōshū, and Tosa troops gave the central government the power to abolish *han* and transform them into prefectures controlled from Tōkyō. In August 1871 it did so, giving *daimyō* generous compensation but reducing the stipends of *samurai*. The road was now clear for further radical changes, such as the introduction of a national education system in 1872, conscription in 1873, the import of foreign technical experts, and the establishment of a monetary land tax in 1873. Japan was well on the way to becoming a modern state.

By 1873 most of the *samurai* leaders had been confirmed in their determination to modernise by a remarkable episode. Led by Iwakura, Ōkubo, and Kido, a 100-strong mission, including most of the outstanding figures in the government, left Japan in December 1871, and did not return until mid-1873. It visited the United States and most of Europe, and its members returned deeply impressed with the power and resources of the West.

In the meantime their colleagues at home, led by Saigō, had been planning an invasion of Korea. Ōkubo and Iwakura, convinced that Japan must place top priority on internal strengthening, opposed them and

The departure from Yokohama of the Iwakura mission in December 1871. Many leaders of the new Meiji government were members of this mission, visiting America and Europe, and learning many of the secrets of Western strength during their year and a half abroad

after a bitter debate the advocates of overseas expansion left the government. Although some mounted uprisings these were easily crushed. Japan was now governed by *samurai* firmly dedicated to modernisation.

5

The Meiji Oligarchs

The group which emerged victorious from the 1873 crisis was to dominate Japanese government for the remaining four decades of the Meiji period. Despite the deaths of Kido and Ōkubo, the original leaders, *samurai* from Satsuma and Chōshū remained in control. Their preponderance was equally marked in the Army, Navy, bureaucracy and police, and attracted bitter criticism. Nevertheless, the closeness of the ruling group was the foundation for remarkable achievements by the Meiji leaders.

Except for its commitment to the aim of *fukoku kyōhei* (rich country, strong army) the Meiji government was bound by no dogma or ideology. On the whole, it was cautious and preferred compromise, but this did not prevent it from making radical changes or acting decisively when it seemed necessary. Abolition of *samurai* special privileges, for example, came only in gradual stages. Yet the government finally achieved its radical objective when in 1876 *samurai* were forbidden to wear swords and their regular stipends were replaced by a single issue of inconvertible government bonds.

Caution and compromise also marked the handling of the vigorous political movement calling for the establishment of a parliament organised by *samurai* leaders from Tosa who, angry at the refusal to invade Korea, had left the government in 1873. The Meiji government might well have

The promulgation of the Meiji Constitution by the Emperor in 1889

suppressed this challenge to its power. Instead, in 1881, the Emperor promised a parliament in nine years' time.

In making this gesture of compromise the Meiji oligarchs were doing nothing which conflicted with their own convictions. They were aware of the need to provide a legitimate channel for the expression of dissent and discontent. They were also conscious that the existing form of government was too personal. It was essential that the Emperor should remain above politics as a symbol of national unity. A constitution would achieve this end by placing responsibility for policies clearly on ministers.

It was Itō Hirobumi from Chōshū who was entrusted with the drafting of the constitution. To prepare himself for the task he travelled to Europe to study the working of parliamentary institutions. Most of Itō's time was spent in Germany where he listened to German constitutional scholars and consulted Bismarck, but the sophisticated document which finally emerged was neatly tailored to his own estimate of Japan's particular requirements. It established a Diet composed of two houses, the lower of which was to be elected, though on a narrow franchise which gave fewer than half a million Japanese the vote, while the upper consisted of three categories— elected representatives of the peers and the highest taxpayers, and imperial nominees. Either house could reject the government's budget, but in that case the previous year's budget would be continued. Cabinet responsibility to the Diet, which would have infringed imperial sovereignty, was conspicuous by its absence. It was an impressive piece of work, even to critically minded Western diplomats. Considering that it was put into operation less than two decades after the end of feudalism, it was as liberal as even the political parties could reasonably expect.

For the next ten years oligarchic cabinets struggled to maintain the upper hand against parties which condemned them as *hambatsu* (*han* cliques) and clamoured for tax reductions and a share in power. In the first election, in 1890, the parties secured an overall majority in the lower house and this they never lost, despite the frequent use of improper methods by the government in later campaigns. (At least twenty-five people were killed and 392 wounded in the 1892 election campaign.)

The government had most of the legal advantages, but the lower house's power to resist budget increases was a trump card at a time when the renewal of Western encroachment on China threatened Japan's interests and made greater military expenditure necessary. The Meiji leaders keenly wanted to avoid national disunity, and some of them were prepared to co-operate again with party leaders, even to the extent of admitting them to ministerial positions. Such arrangements of convenience, however, proved unsatisfactory, and in 1900 Itō reluctantly acknowledged the need for a permanent partnership between parties and oligarchs when he became president of the Seiyūkai Party. Political parties had come of age.

Always present in the minds of the Meiji leaders as they dealt with internal political problems were Japan's foreign relations. Since the Shimonoseki expedition of 1864 the immediate danger of foreign invasion might have loomed less large, but the Meiji leaders could not be certain it would not recur. Nor had Japan emerged from the last troubled years of the Tokugawa period without some encroachment on her independence. Not until 1875 was the Meiji government able to persuade Britain and France to withdraw the troops they had stationed in Yokohama since 1863, and revision of the treaties signed under a sense of duress in 1858 was to take a great deal longer.

The 1858 treaties have generally been termed by Japanese the 'unequal treaties'. They rested on the assumption that Japan was an inferior member of the international community and their provisions were extremely one-sided, relating almost exclusively to foreigners' rights in Japan. The main Japanese grievances were extraterritoriality, which meant that any foreigner accused of any offence, civil or criminal, would be tried in his own consular court; and lack of control over tariff duties, which by a convention signed in 1866 had been generally reduced to five per cent.

The 'unequal treaties' were due for revision after fourteen years. When 1872 arrived, however, the Meiji government found that the Powers required compensation for any concessions they might make and in any case refused to abandon extraterritoriality until Japan had a well-tried Western-style legal system. The task of finding a solution which met the requirements of each country while at the same time satisfying Japanese public opinion was to occupy Meiji governments from 1872 to 1897, and it caused more than one crisis. In 1887 the Foreign Minister, Inoue Kaoru, was forced to resign by public outcry, and two years later his successor, Ōkuma Shigenobu, lost a leg when an ultranationalist threw a bomb at him for proposing that foreigners should serve as judges in some Japanese courts. Eventually, in 1894, Britain, the main stumbling block, agreed to a revised treaty which ended extraterritoriality, and other countries, willingly or otherwise, fell into line.

Treaty revision posed many knotty diplomatic problems, but the basic objective was a simple one, which engaged the support of all Japanese. The same could not be said of the other main foreign policy concerns of the Meiji leaders—relations with Korea and China. These were issues which produced many differences, both about aims and methods.

Some of these differences were revealed in the *Seikan-ron* (Invade Korea Debate), which split the government in 1873. The group led by Ōkubo took the view that Japan must be cautious in her actions, avoiding any measure which was likely to lead to foreign intervention. Against this, Saigō and his supporters advanced what was almost a new version of the *jōi* line. They held that to rely upon diplomacy was to run unnecessary risks. Russia in particular could not be trusted, and only by expanding into Korea could the northern threat be countered.

The debate in 1873 was won by Ōkubo. However, Korea remained a vital area for Japan, both because of its strategic importance and because it was a tributary state of China. As such, it raised a much more complex question. Some Japanese saw China rather like Korea, as an area to be controlled by military force to provide a defensive barrier against the West, but such a view was not held widely. Much more common was the idea of

40

MEIJI JAPAN AND THE FAR EAST

Sino–Japanese co-operation (*Nisshin teikei-ron*). This was supported even by leaders who were concerned to maintain good relations with the West. Its principal advocate was Iwakura. In 1882, he expressed its essence when he wrote: 'Although the decadence of China has reached an extreme point, she is . . . with Japan, almost the only country in the whole of Asia to preserve her independence. Unless we strengthen our barrier of independence by interdependence it will be difficult to ward off the raging billows of Western advance for long.'

This *Nisshin teikei-ron* produced two significant variants. The radical wing of the party movement had little faith in the corrupt and inefficient Manchu dynasty which still, after more than two centuries, governed

41

China, despite having suffered repeated humiliations from Western Powers and accepted infringements on Chinese territory and sovereignty. In their view the cause of Japanese and Asian independence could best be served by Japan giving assistance to popular independence movements in Asia. This was the main intellectual origin of the Pan-Asian movement which was soon to give the Chinese revolutionary leader Sun Yat-sen considerable encouragement.

Somewhere between Iwakura and the radicals stood Fukuzawa Yukichi, the most influential publicist and thinker of Meiji Japan. Although less fervent than the radicals, he shared their doubts about the effectiveness of co-operation with China and Korea as long as these countries remained conservative and backward. Japan, therefore, should 'protect them with arms and encourage them with the pen', but if they were unco-operative and the situation demanded haste it would be justifiable 'to coerce them into progress by force'. Such views were an ominous foretaste of things to come.

For twenty years after the 1873 crisis Japan's policy towards the West reflected Ōkubo's caution and her policy towards China the ideals of Iwakura. This did not prevent her from seeking to improve her position in Korea, but the Meiji government's aims stopped short of seizing control of Korea. Had it wished to do so, it had the opportunity in late 1884, when China was involved in war with France. A pro-Japanese faction staged a short-lived *coup d'état* in the Korean capital, but Itō and Inoue rejected French overtures. Good relations with China were more important to them than advantages in Korea or alliance with a major European power.

Ten years later, in July 1894, a Japanese government again headed by Itō went to war with China over the question of Korean reform. This dramatic development did not, however, represent a change in basic attitude, but was essentially a response to changed circumstances arising out of European power politics. In 1891, the Russian government decided to build the Trans-Siberian Railway, which would enable it to send at speed large numbers of men to the Far East. Korean reform became an urgent necessity if the peninsula were not to be a helpless prey of Russian ambition. If China would not co-operate then Chinese influence would have to be removed. A serious revolt in Korea in 1894 gave Japan the excuse to act. China, having predictably rejected Japan's proposals for reform, found herself at war.

Few Westerners predicted a Japanese victory, but within a few months

An artist's view of the Japanese Army's entry into Mukden ▶
in 1905 during the Russo–Japanese War

Japanese armies in Korea and Manchuria were everywhere supreme and the Japanese navy commanded the sea. Early in 1895 a peace treaty was signed at Shimonoseki. China withdrew from Korea, agreed to pay a large indemnity, gave Japan substantial commercial rights, and ceded to her the island of Taiwan and the Liaotung peninsula in southern Manchuria. At once Russia stepped in. Supported by Germany and France, she demanded that the Liaotung peninsula be handed back in the interests of peace. This Triple Intervention was a bitter blow to Japan, yet the government dared not refuse the Russian demand. Three years later Russia secured a lease on Port Arthur and important railway rights in the same Liaotung peninsula.

Events now moved inexorably towards a trial of strength. Japan was determined to put an end to Russia's interference in Korea and to her military occupation of Manchuria for which the anti-foreign Boxer Uprising of 1900 in China had provided a pretext. Once alliance had been made with Britain, in January 1902, there was no need to fear attack from Russia's ally, France. Nevertheless, until December 1903 the Japanese government genuinely sought a compromise with Russia. Only when negotiations repeatedly proved futile did it take the decision for war.

The struggle was a desperate one, involving huge loss of life. Port Arthur only surrendered after a long siege and although in February–March 1905 General Ōyama won the important battle of Mukden, it was not until the Russian Baltic fleet was overwhelmed by Admiral Tōgō in the Tsushima Straits that Russia agreed to peace negotiations. Even then, it was Japan, financially exhausted, which sought American help in starting talks, and she was unable to impose all her terms on her adversary. Nevertheless, the aims for which she had resorted to war were achieved. By the Treaty of Portsmouth of 5 September 1905, Russia completely withdrew from Korean affairs and her leases in south Manchuria were transferred to Japan.

By 1905 the Meiji leaders had realised their chief objective of establishing Japan as a strong, independent nation. For the next few years Japan was to enjoy greater security and stability than at any other time in her modern history.

6

Economic Modernisation

The dramatic victories over China and Russia would have been impossible if Japan had not experienced an economic transformation. As the Meiji leaders constantly emphasised with the slogan *fukoku kyōhei* (rich country, strong army), military capability was dependent on the development of national resources. While still far behind the leading Western nations in 1905, Japan was well on the way to becoming an industrial power.

This increase in economic strength would have surprised many earlier observers. In 1879, for instance, one French diplomat wrote that 'Japan is surely marching towards anarchy.' He was by no means alone in pouring scorn on Japan's efforts.

Leaders of today's newly independent nations might take heart from the fact that these gloomy forecasts proved so wrong. However, they would probably find the pace of the Japanese transformation depressing. There was no sudden 'economic miracle' in the nineteenth century. In 1913 manufacturing industry still accounted for no more than one-seventh of Japan's labour force and of this one-seventh roughly one-third were self-employed. Of 32,290 factories in 1909 less than one-third were equipped with power machinery and more than half of those in private ownership were really workshops employing fewer than ten people. Before the First World War, in fact, the major sources of Japan's national wealth were

45

In the Tokugawa period the colour print was developed by many outstanding artists.
This view by Hiroshige (1797–1858) of the Tamagawa (Jewel River) near Edo (Tōkyō)
shows something of the picturesque quality of the country before modernisation

agriculture, which still involved well over half the working population but had increased its productivity considerably; traditional industries and handicrafts, most of which had expanded to keep pace with the rising population and a fairly general improvement of living standards; and the more modern light industries, notably silk-reeling and cotton-spinning, which relied on cheap labour and which needed much less capital to introduce Western technology than heavy industry.

It would be wrong, however, to ignore completely the development of modern heavy industry. Its initial stages were marked by enormous financial and technical difficulties, but after the Sino–Japanese War its rate of expansion began to accelerate. Heavy industry also played a major role in the general development of commerce. Shipbuilding and railway construction are obvious examples. Nevertheless, even in the field of transport it was the extension of the old-fashioned road system, the invention of the rickshaw (replaced by the bicycle after 1900), and the proliferation of carts which had the greatest immediate economic importance.

In considering Japan's economic growth the first point which should be made is that Japan possessed very few natural resources. Coal and iron, the great necessities of the age, existed, but not in abundance. Of the few natural assets Japan possessed perhaps the chief was her climate, which favoured the rearing of silkworms. By an extraordinary stroke of good fortune the ending of Japan's isolation coincided with the spread of a disease known as pébrine through the European silkworm industry. Many enterprising Japanese made unexpected profits from the large-scale export of silk and silkworm eggs, and these exports offset a potentially adverse balance of trade.

One other asset should be mentioned. Japan was a small country, no part of which was remote from the coast. A few hundred miles of railway line could bring the major economic areas along the east coast into close contact with each other, and a few thousand miles could ensure that the whole country was involved in the national market. Because of its size it was also capable of government from the centre. Old *han* loyalties might continue in muted form but there could be no tendency towards regional separatism. This had a significant bearing on the political stability which economic development required.

Japan's emergence as an economic power was also affected by world conditions and foreign attitudes. The technological gap between Europe and Japan in the 1870s, for instance, was not so great as it is between developed and underdeveloped countries today. In time, the Japanese could hope to bridge it. Nor were they without practical assistance. Japanese historians have discovered the names of nearly 1,500 foreigners, almost half of them British, who played a role in the introduction of industrial technology. The importance attached to their skills can be seen in the fact that they were often paid more than government ministers.

Because the danger of external political control seemed great, the Meiji leaders dared not rely on foreign capital to finance their industrial projects. Apart from two loans amounting to £3,400,000, floated in London in 1870 and 1873, Japan borrowed nothing until after the Sino–Japanese War. Rather than risk foreign interference, the Japanese government resigned itself to squeezing a resentful peasantry. The 'unequal treaties' of 1858 aggravated this situation for they made it impossible to increase government revenue through higher import or export duties. They also handicapped Japanese development by preventing the government from using tariffs to protect new industries against foreign competition. No alternative was left but a policy of selective subsidies to favoured companies, which was not only unfair but bred an unhealthy reliance on the government among the leaders of new industry.

The real key to Japan's economic transformation lay in the Tokugawa

The first graduates of Tōkyō Imperial University, 1885. Mainly of *samurai* background in the Meiji period, the majority of Tōkyō University graduates entered the bureaucracy and helped to provide the stability and guidance necessary for economic development

heritage. Just as traditional industries were responsible for most of the increased production of the new era, so traditional values provided the motivating force for many Japanese. Foremost among these values was nationalism. *Fukoku kyōhei* was the rallying cry for most Japanese who undertook improvements or ventured into new fields. Industry became an aspect of patriotism. This profession of faith by a successful Meiji business leader was typical: 'Even if I lose the capital I have invested in a business, I do not regret it in the slightest, since business (as a whole) has gained . . . Once an enterprise has been launched, society ultimately benefits.'

Nationalism also involved the *samurai* in economic development. As the most highly educated group within Japanese society, they were best equipped to grapple with Western ideas and techniques, but hitherto they

48

had regarded commerce and manufacturing as occupations beneath their dignity. The government's emphasis on building up the country's economic strength, however, made such activities respectable, and provided the means of converting a class which had lost its purpose into a major national asset. From their ranks emerged roughly half of Meiji Japan's business leaders.

The *samurai* contribution to stability was no less important than their direct participation in the economy. Most *samurai* followed their *daimyō* in transferring their allegiance to the Emperor. The agencies upon which the government chiefly depended for the maintenance of order—the Army, the police, and the prefectural governors—were all staffed in the upper ranks almost exclusively by *samurai*. Even in education a large proportion of teachers were of *samurai* background.

It was also an essentially *samurai* government which decreed the extinction of feudalism and introduced most of the trappings of a modern state. As part of this effort it allotted about five per cent of its revenues during its first thirteen years to industrial investment. In some industries, such as silk-reeling, it established model factories; in others it subsidised private businesses; and in heavy or strategic industries such as railways and mines, where the investment risks were too high for individuals, the government itself pioneered in the application of new technology by setting up state companies. The results of direct government enterprise were not spectacular. Losses were frequently incurred and after 1881 most government-owned mines and factories were sold off to private capitalists at a low price. Nevertheless, the seeds had been sown of Japan's later transformation into a major industrial power.

Crucial though it was, government initiative in economic matters would not, by itself, have been sufficient to transform the economy had not a considerable proportion of the population given its support. This was by no means inevitable: for example, many of the old-fashioned merchants of Tōkyō and Ōsaka failed to respond positively to the new challenge until the late 1880s. During the Tokugawa period there had, however, grown up a class of wealthy peasants ready to exploit any commercial opportunities which presented themselves. It was men of this sort who planted more mulberry trees to feed larger numbers of silkworms and established contacts with foreign merchants.

The initiative, adaptability, and capital resources of such individuals were part of the Tokugawa legacy. So too, was a high standard of literacy.

The Mitsubishi dockyard at Nagasaki in about 1888

The ability of over a quarter of the population to read provided a good foundation for the introduction of a national education system which by 1900 was giving over ninety per cent of Japanese children the basic knowledge and discipline essential to a modern labour force. Equally traditional was population control. Though this was gradually relaxed, the rise in the birth-rate did not get out of hand. In this Japan resembled Britain during the Industrial Revolution rather than nineteenth-century China or the underdeveloped countries of the twentieth century. There was an abundant supply of cheap labour, but the population increased slightly more slowly than the production of food and goods. No large discontented proletariat was created which might have threatened Japan's political stability.

It was due in part to the relative population stability that the Japanese family system survived the transition from Tokugawa to Meiji intact. The family system greatly softened the impact of industrialisation. Most of the employees in the new industries were the daughters or second sons of peasants and were found places generally through family contacts. If they

Most of the workers in Japan's early textile factories were women

did not work diligently they would shame their parents—or their parents'
landlord—and jeopardise their chances of future employment. However,
the family system also influenced the behaviour of employers. Just as
employees were supposed to conduct themselves like good children, so
employers were expected to give their workers paternal attention. Even if
these ideals were rarely realised, they did help to counteract the impersonal
nature of industrialisation. It was possible for a prominent labour leader,
Suzuki Bunji, to write in 1918 that because Japan enjoyed familial-type
relations rather than individualism, the problem of industrial relations
was different from that in the West. In Japan, he proclaimed, 'The
capitalist works and creates the facilities that promote the happiness and
well-being of the workers. He not only provides facilities for the education,
health, and recreation of the workers, but also for death, sickness, and old
age. He provides housing and encourages (the habit of) saving. In doing
all this he is like a kind and loving parent and loves his children: between
them there is no discord, no (problem of) obligations, but rather a spirit of
mutual trust. On this basis the factory becomes exactly like a family.' It is
statements like this which have led some scholars to conclude, with
pardonable exaggeration, that 'Traditional Japanese culture, instead of
being swept aside by industrialism, has assimilated it.'

51

7

The New Society
of Meiji Japan

None of the *samurai* who argued in the 1860s about the effects of opening Japan fully to the outside world could have foreseen exactly what Japanese society and everyday life would be like by the end of the century. If they had, they would have been struck most immediately, particularly in the main cities, by the changes in the physical character of Japan.

The most obvious changes were those brought about by Western science and technology. Along the Tōkaidō, the famous eastern seaboard route from Edo to Ōsaka which skirted Mount Fuji and had provided favourite views for the artists of the Tokugawa period, telegraph poles now sprouted, with railway tracks by their side. Indeed, no town of any size was without its railway connection, and journeys which had taken weeks in former years could now be achieved in days. In and around Tōkyō, Yokohama, Ōsaka, Kōbe and Kyōto, trams circulated, usually very crowded and already, like gas lighting, an accepted part of city life. Elsewhere in Japan the long hours after dark had been brightened by the use of imported kerosene oil for lamps. Factory chimneys belched smoke, not only in urban areas but in some country districts as well.

These technological innovations were not the only striking changes in Japanese everyday life. Partly from a desire to impress Western countries with their modernity, partly from a fascination with what was new and

This photograph of the 1870s reflects the current desire to emulate Western fashions

exotic, many Japanese in the open ports and cities began to experiment with Western-style clothing from about 1870. Not infrequently their first efforts provoked ridicule, as a newly acquired top-hat or frock-coat was combined with a traditional *hakama* (divided skirt) or with two protruding *samurai* swords. But by the end of the century Western-style suits had become standard for officials and businessmen. Even in the countryside the new era brought significant changes. In particular, the brighter colours which had formerly been reserved for festivals gradually spread into everyday costume, and the introduction of cheap cotton clothing rendered the burdensome weaving of uncomfortable hemp garments unnecessary.

Changes in fashion were not confined to dress. In the villages some officials were given certificates of merit for promoting Western hair-styles,

A street in Tōkyō's central Ginza district in 1905

and in many towns zealous officials prohibited mixed bathing in public bath-houses. In 1873 the government even risked considerable opposition by changing from the Chinese to the Western calendar, and by as far as possible substituting the seven-day week, with Sunday a holiday, for the traditional ten-day cycle.

The passion for 'civilisation and enlightenment' (*bummei kaika*) also extended to the realm of food. In 1872 the Emperor was persuaded to eat beef for the first time, and meat-eating and milk-drinking were promoted, with reasonable success, by the government, which experimented by introducing cattle and sheep, mainly into Hokkaidō. Several new fruits were introduced, among them the peach, pear, apple and navel orange. They represented some recompense for the export of so many varieties of Japanese flowers, shrubs, and trees to the West. Among new beverages beer, coffee, and Indian tea were the most popular. As important for the average Japanese as any of these new acquisitions, however, was the greatly increased consumption of sugar—formerly a highly priced luxury—of soya sauce, and of rice.

The Japanese standard of living probably improved during the Meiji period. It is true that many unfortunate peasants, unable to pay the new monetary land tax, were forced into tenancy, but it is equally true that the end of isolation reduced the danger of mass starvation by permitting food imports when harvests were bad. However, there is no absolute standard by which one can measure improved levels of nutrition against the longer hours probably worked by most Japanese. In any case, numerous other changes affecting Japanese society must be taken into account.

The most important of these changes was that of legal status. With the dismantling of the feudal structure of government in 1871 restrictions on the freedom of movement of both *samurai* and peasants disappeared. In the same year, the Meiji government awarded certificates of landownership to those who were responsible for the payment of taxes on particular pieces of land, namely, the peasant landlords or owner-cultivators.

The old class distinctions had now almost disappeared, and the process was completed with the abandonment of the old four-class system of *samurai*, peasant, artisan and merchant. By the twentieth century the only group which suffered social discrimination was the *eta*, or *burakumin*, a pariah class traditionally shunned by other Japanese.

What they gained in the way of legal equality many peasants would doubtless have been willing to give up in return for the removal of a new burden. As citizens they were now liable to conscription. Many of the minor peasant revolts which marked the early 1870s were due to resentment at this unanticipated obligation. In the long run, however, conscription widened the young conscript's horizons and stimulated his ambition, as well as promoting a sense of equality since all conscripts were treated in the same way.

One other important effect of military training was the indoctrination of the young soldier with the idea of service to the state and reverence for the Emperor. This accentuated the teaching given in the new education system, which was providing at least six years' instruction to all children by 1907. In the new schools ethics, conceived as an amalgamation of emperor-worship, patriotism, and filial piety, was given an important place. Nevertheless the need for Japan to catch up with the West meant that a fairly general education was aimed at; when imperial universities were established in the 1880s and 1890s they were charged with 'the offering of instruction in carrying on thorough investigation in the arts and sciences to meet the needs of the state.'

One of the greatest of the educational problems facing Japan was the dissemination of up-to-date Western knowledge among Japanese educators. It was here that such men as Fukuzawa Yukichi were indispensable. An ex-Dutch scholar, he established a newspaper and founded Keiō University. His most important work, however, was the writing, in straightforward language, of books on almost every subject, incorporating his understanding of, and deductions from, Western doctrines and practices.

Books were not the only means of spreading information in Meiji Japan, however. Inspired by the various English treaty-port newspapers, a vigorous Japanese press sprang up in the decade following the Meiji Restoration. Circulations remained in the low thousands until after the Russo–Japanese War, but they were often passed around from family to family. For those in Tōkyō who were interested and could afford them, there were also journals dealing with serious and controversial issues.

Among these journals were two—*Nihonjin* (Japanese) and *Kokumin no Tomo* (The Nation's Friend), which expressed the fundamental concerns of the younger generation. The basic issue confronting them was how to reconcile Western superiority with Japanese tradition and pride. Conscious though they were of the benefits which Japan's opening to the West had brought, the contributors to *Nihonjin* nevertheless felt that there were certain Japanese traditions of which they could be proud. Against them the other group of young intellectuals advocated complete Westernisation and argued that Japan should earn the right to pride by outstripping Western nations in progress, including progress in warfare. Between them the two viewpoints represented the dilemma which many Japanese would continue to feel.

The young were not the only ones in the 1880s who were worried about Japan's cultural identity. Not only had Western-style drama, novels, and painting become popular, but a society had been set up to urge the replacement of ideographs by the Western alphabet. Even more disturbing were strong rumours that the government was contemplating the adoption of Christianity as an official religion of the state in order to impress foreign countries.

To many Japanese this seemed a very serious threat. Both Buddhism and Confucianism had suffered a distinct decline, at least among the better educated. Shintō, it is true, retained its hold on popular feeling, but it was not strong intellectually. There was clearly a chance for Christianity to repeat its success of three centuries earlier—indeed, soon after it received practical toleration in 1873 the number of converts began to increase. By 1889 there were 34,000 Christians in Japan, many of *samurai* background.

In the event, Christianity did not become an official religion, and its rapid advance of the 1880s slowed down in the following decades. Its check can be attributed in part to the slow progress of treaty revision negotiations, which turned the campaign to introduce aspects of Western culture some-what sour, but more significantly it stemmed from the ending of political and social uncertainty in the 1890s. As in the sixteenth century, Christianity had thrived when rapid unsettling changes were taking place and people had not found satisfactory new roles. Once a stable social and governmental framework had been established, Christianity began to seem more a danger to Japan's basic inherited values. 'In Japan loyalty and filial piety are the focal points of morality,' stated a book entitled *Against the Official Recognition of Christianity* (1899). 'But in Christianity the focal points are on God and Jesus, and loyalty and filial piety are denied. Those who deny loyalty and filial piety are unlearned people who have not read the classics and who do not know the beauty of our national family system. They have been swept into the current of individual selfishness.'

The feelings expressed here were widely shared. They show that for all the changes of the Meiji years a strong core of traditional attitudes still persisted. Nowhere was this more important than in family relationships. Although foreign legal advisers had played a prominent part in the drafting of the Civil Code, the latter contained some provisions deriving from Japanese custom which differed significantly from Western law. It was laid down, for instance, that a son's first duty was to maintain his parents rather than his wife or children; there was full acceptance of the use of adoption as a means of preserving a family name; permission of the family-head was necessary for any marriage, and marriage between only children was prohibited because it would mean the extinction of one family; at least half a family's property had to be passed to the eldest son, and in practice younger children got very little.

Much of this was not merely traditional but more particularly a part of *samurai* tradition. Just as businessmen were being led to regard themselves as modern *samurai*, protecting the country with economic weapons, so the ordinary citizen was having *samurai* standards imposed on him. Even where they were not directly imposed they were sometimes copied, as when marriages became almost invariably arranged through go-betweens, rather than through the freer traditions which had been practised in most Tokugawa villages. At another level, every Japanese child was being incul-cated with ideals of loyalty to the Emperor which were also closer to the *bushidō* tradition than to non-*samurai* values. The continuing strength of this tradition was to have repercussions on Japan's development in the twentieth century.

57

8

Taishō Japan

When the Emperor Meiji died in 1912 it was as much a landmark in modern Japanese history as the death of Queen Victoria had been in British. Immediately afterwards the Japanese public was jolted by the suicide of General Nogi, a hero of the Russo–Japanese War. His *hara-kiri* was widely interpreted as a warning against new trends in Japanese society. It was a reminder that Japan's existing stability might be endangered unless she could solve the problems which Meiji success had produced. In particular, there seemed to be the threat of a spread of materialistic attitudes and a growth of class conflict. In the hope of giving a moral lead the new Emperor's advisers chose the word *Taishō* (Great Righteousness) for his reign-name. Almost at once, however, the clash of ambitions produced Japan's most serious domestic crisis for at least two decades.

At the root of this crisis was the question of who should succeed to the power wielded by the Meiji oligarchs. The men who had steered Japan through the ending of isolation and the establishment of a modern state were by 1912 either dead or too old to bear the burdens of office. They now wished to pass the responsibilities of government on to the most outstanding of their younger supporters. Nevertheless, these elder statesmen, or *genrō*, had no intention of parting with all their power. All important decisions still had to be taken in accordance with their views. Of these distinguished but wily political manipulators, the most influential were Itō, until he was assassinated by a Korean in 1909, and Yamagata Aritomo, who, more than any other soldier, had shaped the new Japanese army, and who had twice been Prime Minister. Both were from Chōshū, but their rivalry was keen.

For eleven years after Itō's resignation in 1901, the office of Prime Minister alternated between Katsura Tarō, a Chōshū general and protégé of Yamagata, and Saionji Kimmochi, a sophisticated court noble who was appointed as much because he represented Itō as because he had succeeded him as president of the Seiyūkai Party. To outward appearances it seemed that the *genrō* had successfully handed over the succession to like-minded men. Behind the scenes, however, a struggle developed between Katsura and Hara Kei, political director of the Seiyūkai, with Saionji in the middle. By 1911, Hara's skill and the Seiyūkai's firm majority in the Diet had put so much pressure on Katsura that he retired from active politics.

In December 1912, however, the Army refused to supply a new minister to Saionji's cabinet unless funds were made available for two new divisions, and Saionji was forced to resign. Katsura now returned to politics, attempting by bribery and other inducements to break up the Seiyūkai and create a new government party loyal to himself. This was the same dream which Itō had cherished, but Katsura's hopes were even more short-lived. When the Diet met in February 1913, Katsura was confronted with a determined opposition which made government impossible. Conscious that Yamagata disapproved of his bid to associate the government with a political party, Katsura resigned. Before the end of the year he was dead.

The Taishō Political Crisis proved that the Diet could not be ignored or manipulated. Nevertheless, although the majority party was able to use its powers of obstruction to impose some of its policies on governments, prime ministers continued to be chosen by the Emperor in accordance with the *genrō*'s advice.

This compromise arrangement lasted until the end of the First World War. By that time, however, the parties were becoming impatient for full party cabinets and the *genrō* were growing less active. The year 1922 saw the death of Yamagata, the most influential of the original *genrō*, and after 1924 there remained only one second-generation elder statesman, Prince Saionji, who had retired from active politics in 1913. The long era of *genrō* politics was over.

Equally important, however, for the party politicians was the First

A meeting of three of Taishō Japan's leading party politicians in 1916. On the left is Katō Kōmei; next to him Hara Kei, and on the extreme right Inukai Ki

World War. The Japanese people were not unaware in 1918 that it was the most democratic countries which were winning. Democratic ideas enjoyed a considerable vogue in Japan, and not only democratic ideas, for the Russian Revolution also made a real impact, even if it shocked most Japanese.

In some ways the decade following the war is reminiscent of the *bummei kaika* period of the 1870s in its re-awakened responsiveness to new Western ideas and practices. One example was the appearance of the *mobo* (modern boy) and *moga* (modern girl), both displaying enthusiasm for current Western fashions and crazes. At a deeper level the works of Tolstoy, Dostoevsky and other serious European writers became influential among the growing number of young intellectuals produced by the universities. New currents such as these helped to create a new mood, more critical of the old order, which made political change easier to achieve.

The war also gave indirect economic assistance to the party movement. The preoccupation of the main European countries with their great struggle opened up a trade vacuum in eastern Asia which Japan was well placed to fill. Industrialists and businessmen acquired a greater sense of importance and confidence, and the parties were the natural channel by which they could exert greater influence on government.

More immediately, the wartime boom brought inflation. With it arose working-class discontent, which suddenly flared up into mass protest in

60

many parts of the country when the price of rice rocketed in 1918. It was largely because of this unprecedented popular unrest that Yamagata was compelled to put aside his life-long hostility to party cabinets and recommend Hara Kei as Prime Minister.

The foundation of the Hara ministry in September 1918 inaugurated a period of nearly fourteen years when party cabinets were normal. Hara's own career, however, was cut short by assassination in 1921, and the Seiyūkai Party then split into two factions. For a brief period, between 1922 and 1924, there were three non-party cabinets headed successively by an admiral, an ex-bureaucrat peer, and another admiral, but the Seiyūkai and its chief rival, the Kenseikai, were now too strong to be pushed into a subordinate role. In 1924 a coalition party cabinet was formed by Katō Kōmei, leader of the Kenseikai, to be followed in 1926 by that of Wakatsuki Reijirō, another Kenseikai leader. Thereafter a two-party system began to emerge, with General Tanaka Giichi heading a Seiyūkai cabinet from 1927 to 1929, Hamaguchi Yūkō, a Minseitō (the name given to the re-shaped Kenseikai after 1927) ministry from 1929 to 1931, and Inukai Ki, a Seiyūkai government from 1931 to 1932.

The 1920s were the high point of constitutional development in pre-war Japan and are often called the period of 'Taishō democracy'. There were, it is true, some signs of greater liberalism and increasing popular participation in politics. After several cautious reductions in the franchise, voting rights were eventually extended in 1925 to all men over twenty-five. Some legislation was passed to remedy the worst factory conditions, and in 1925 the Katō ministry succeeded in reducing the Army from twenty-one to seventeen divisions. Finally, throughout the 1920s, but particularly during the Kenseikai/Minseitō cabinets, Japanese diplomacy revealed an exceptional international-mindedness.

The parties had a less progressive side, however. The extension of the franchise, for example, was followed by a Peace Preservation Law under which some left-wing parties with moderate programmes were permitted, but Communists and anarchists were harshly persecuted. The established parties could not afford to carry liberalism too far—they themselves were too closely identified with business and landlord interests to be confident of mass support at a time of growing class consciousness.

The most notorious aspect of party politics was corruption. Scandals involving the acceptance of bribes by Diet members became increasingly common during the Taishō period. No less damaging to the politicians'

Taishō democracy at its highest point. A speech in favour of political rights for women in 1928. Note, however, the conspicuous presence of the police

reputation was the parties' dependence on vested interests. By the 1920s it was normal for party leadership to fall to men whose business connections allowed them to give their supporters financial help during campaigns. Such links made it easy to argue that the parties were concerned more with particular interests than the national good.

It was not only the parties' own limitations which prevented Taishō Japan from being genuinely democratic. Even more of a barrier were the constitutional limitations on the power of the Lower House. Although it had become necessary during the 1920s for the Prime Minister to be a party leader, this did not mean that party cabinets could govern as they wished. Court officials, informal imperial advisers, the Privy Council, and the House of Peers were all capable of exerting a powerful influence on government. So, too, were the Army and Navy, both of which enjoyed a semi-independent position. Even better placed was the bureaucracy. For the drafting of legislation and the implementation of policy, cabinets were in the hands of their highly educated and trained civil servants. It was significant that many top politicians were themselves ex-bureaucrats.

This dispersion of real power among several élite groups was yet another example of the peculiar interaction between modernisation and Japanese tradition. On the modern side a centralised state had been created, but the focus of this state was a traditional figure—the Emperor—who was bound both by history and training to remain essentially a symbol. Such a system carried no guarantee of firm, united leadership. The Meiji leaders had provided such leadership with their dominance of the Army, Navy and bureaucracy, and their own national prestige, but they had been unable to hand over their controlling influence to their chosen successors. The parties might seem to have inherited the oligarchs' mantle, but in reality the old tradition of intricate division of power dating from the Fujiwara age had reasserted itself. Only if there were a new national crisis would a more unified government be likely to appear.

If such a crisis did occur, however, it would not be the parties who profited from it. At home they were associated with class interests and were in no position to secure national unity. In foreign policy they had been internationalist, and because they had reduced both the Army and Navy they were open to the charge that they were placing economy before the protection of Japan's national interests. The growing number of ultra-nationalists in Japan during the 1920s was an ominous sign. Like the *samurai* loyalists of the 1860s, these 'double patriots' saw in Western ideas and the Western world a threat to Japan's security and national character. If the Japanese people as a whole should come to share their views, the gains made by the parties would be in jeopardy.

9

Japan in World Politics (1905-30)

In 1905 it seemed as if Japan had solved the problems which had made the Meiji oligarchs fear for the country's independence. She had established herself as a major Power, and by 1910 had brought Korea under her full control. In one important way, however, Japan continued to feel vulnerable. Her national interests were all bound up in the Far East, yet the alignment of the other Powers in the area was mainly dependent on European power-politics. While European rivalries might work to Japan's advantage, they could equally well produce a coalition hostile to Japan. Japanese statesmen could not easily forget the Triple Intervention.

In this situation many Japanese still clung to the belief that the Chinese would come to recognise their common interest with Japan in resisting the further advance of the Western Powers, and would be grateful for Japanese help and leadership. There was some support for this view in Japan's popularity about the time of the Russo–Japanese War when perhaps 8,000 Chinese were given the rudiments of a modern, often a military, education in Japan. Nevertheless, there were already signs that Japan's concern with China might be self-defeating. Japan's take-over of the rights which Russia had extorted from China in south Manchuria might be accepted by a powerless China in 1905. Before long, however, it would be treated by the growing Chinese nationalist movement as a mark of Japan's conversion to imperialism. At the same time Japan's victory over Russia and China's increasingly obvious weakness were altering the Japanese image of China. The feeling was becoming widespread in Japan that the relationship between Japan and China must be unequal, for the time being at any rate. For all China's immediate difficulties, few Chinese nationalists could stomach this.

The immediate effect of the Russo–Japanese War was the replacement of confrontation by cautious co-operation between the two powers. Their rapprochement in 1907 not only removed the fear of a war of revenge, but it marked the two countries' willingness to co-operate in maintaining their Manchurian privileges against challenge from America and China. Altogether there were four agreements between Japan and Russia between 1907 and 1916. On the eve of the Russian Revolution their relationship was as important to Japan as the alliance with Britain.

In contrast to relations with Russia, Anglo–Japanese relations became less harmonious. There were the beginnings of rivalry over spheres of influence in China, and during the 1911 revolution there the two allies adopted different attitudes. While many Japanese radicals urged support of the Chinese revolutionaries, the Saionji government, influenced by Yamagata's fear of revolution, advocated the acceptance of constitutional government by the Manchu dynasty. Without consulting her ally, however, Britain worked, much more effectively, for a completely new government under the supposed strong man, Yuan Shih-k'ai, who was known to be hostile to Japan.

In view of Japan's diplomatic failure during the Chinese revolution, it was not entirely surprising that she sought to take advantage of the First World War to strengthen her Far Eastern position. Immediately following the outbreak of conflict Japan declared war on Germany and took over by force the privileges which Germany had extorted from China in the Shantung peninsula. Then, at the beginning of 1915, the Foreign Minister, Katō Kōmei, decided to have Germany's rights legally transferred to Japan and at the same time establish a special position for Japan in China. The result was the notorious 'Twenty-One Demands' episode.

In actual fact, Japan only made fifteen demands on the Chinese government of Yuan Shih-k'ai. The remaining six points, which included the most far-reaching, were 'wishes', and were finally dropped. The Japanese aim was two-fold. Recognising that Western imperialism would not vanish from China, Katō sought to improve Japan's economic position

Sun Yat-sen asking for Japanese support for the Chinese revolutionaries at a banquet
in Osaka in March 1913. Sun is third from the left of those standing

there, particularly in Manchuria, where much money had been invested in
the Japanese-controlled South Manchurian Railway Company. This part
of the 'Twenty-One Demands' was resented by China and the Powers, but
was little different from other encroachments by various Powers on
China's rights. Yuan Shih-k'ai was finally forced to accept the demands
when Katō issued an ultimatum in May 1915.

The other side of the 'Twenty-One Demands' reflected Japanese
concern with China as the first line of Japan's own defence. Thus, one
demand was that 'with the object of effectively preserving the territorial
integrity of China' the Chinese government should engage 'not to cede or
lease to a third Power any harbour, bay, or island along the coast of
China'. Katō also requested that Japanese should be appointed as political,
financial, and military advisers. Many historians have regarded this as
Japan's first attempt to turn China into a satellite, foreshadowing the
aggression of the 1930s, but it should be remembered that Japan herself
had modernised with the help of foreign advisers, including military
advisers, and it is worth noting that one Japanese adviser already employed

by Yuan Shih-k'ai did his best to undermine the 'Twenty-One Demands' by appealing to Yamagata.

Although most of the 'Twenty-One Demands' were accepted, Katō's diplomacy was condemned by Yamagata and many other Japanese. Not only had it defeated one of its main objects by totally alienating the Chinese government and Chinese political opinion, but it had also caused friction with America and suspicion in Britain.

During the remaining years of the First World War Japanese policy was aimed at remedying this situation. On the one hand, Japan sought, and gained, the Allies' acquiescence in the fait accompli by sending submarines to convoy Allied ships in the Mediterranean. On the other hand, the Japanese government, and particularly the Army, secretly worked for the overthrow of Yuan Shih-k'ai. When the latter died in 1916 China was already out of his control and falling into the hands of regional warlords. One of these, Tuan Chi-jui, was sympathetic to Japan, and Japanese money helped him to establish himself in Peking.

By the end of the First World War Japan seemed to have consolidated her Far Eastern position. Despite official British and French support for Japan's 1915 gains at the Versailles Peace Conference, however, it became increasingly clear that deep resentment and suspicion had been aroused. It was significant that Japan was unable to secure the insertion of a clause accepting the general principle of racial equality in the Versailles Treaty.

Loss of international respectability was that much more serious because the Russian Revolution of 1917 had deprived Japan of one of her major allies and given her instead a dangerous neighbour. In an ill-considered attempt to overthrow the Bolshevik government or set up a puppet state in eastern Siberia, Japan participated in an Allied expedition to rescue Czech troops in Siberia in 1918. The large Japanese contingent remained until 1922, long after the departure of the rest, but succeeded only in squandering many lives and much money.

The third threat to Japan's position was the rise of Chinese nationalism. Popular feeling against Japan and the Versailles Treaty exploded in the May Fourth Movement of 1919 in Peking and other Chinese cities. Before long the Tuan Chi-jui faction was ousted from Peking and Japan faced a hostile Chinese government as well as an angry people.

Japan's adjustment to this new situation was surprisingly swift, and much of the credit should go to Hara Kei. Abandoning the ideas of a special political relationship with China or military dominance of the

Japanese forces attacking German-held Tsingtao in China in 1914

Far East, he recognised that Japan must return to her pre-war priority of cautious co-operation. The idealistic mood reflected in much of the peace settlement and in the setting up of a League of Nations meant that blatant imperialism and special alliances were no longer practicable. In the 1921–2 Washington Conference called by America, therefore, Japan entered fully into the new 'Washington system' for the Far East. She agreed to a battleship limitation which meant that she could have only three-fifths of the capacity of either Britain or the USA; signed a Nine-Power Treaty pledging respect for Chinese territorial integrity and sympathy for China's national aspirations; and accepted the ending of the alliance with Britain which had incurred much American resentment.

During the 1920s Japan found the 'Washington system' reasonably satisfactory. By restricting the other Powers' activities in the Far East it helped to safeguard Japanese security. Under the guidance of Baron Shidehara Kijūrō, who served as Foreign Minister from 1924 to 1927 and from 1929 to 1931, Japan observed the new rules of diplomacy. In particular, Shidehara's reaction to attacks on Japanese in China was very mild and compared strikingly with Britain's use of force to protect British nationals and British interests. At the end of the 1920s the possibility of a breach with the Western Powers and an invasion of China seemed remote.

10

Crisis at
Home and Abroad

It was in the 1930s that Japan was to show that despite more than half a century of modernisation she had not yet achieved real maturity. As in some European countries, the strains of rapid industrialisation combined with the international uncertainties to produce a fierce reaction against the policies of the preceding years. The six hectic years which culminated in the Army mutiny of 26 February 1936 were to decide which of the alternative approaches would take their place.

Well before 1936 a revolution had taken place in Japanese diplomacy. Ironically it was a hard-won victory for Shidehara's diplomatic policy which set in train the series of events which were to end in the rejection of internationalism. In 1930 the Minseitō cabinet of 'Lion' Hamaguchi overrode the Navy's plan to improve Japan's naval ratio and signed the London Naval Treaty, which continued the system laid down at Washington in 1922. Great indignation was aroused among ultranationalists, and Hamaguchi was fatally wounded by an outraged youth later in the year. His firmness in reducing naval expenditure, however, did not augur well for the Army, which was insisting that no economies could be made so long as Japanese encountered discrimination in Manchuria and the prospect existed of expropriation of Japanese interests by the new Nationalist government of China. While peace continued, however, the

Army could not expect much support from public opinion.

In this situation the Army Minister and Chief of Staff could hardly be expected to condemn too severely any action by Army officers which, by provoking hostilities, lent justification to their claims. Already in 1928 young and middle-ranking officers of the 10,400-strong Japanese Kwantung Army stationed in Manchuria to protect the South Manchurian Railway had attempted to keep the region politically separate from China and to establish Japanese dominance by assassinating Chang Tso-lin, the Chinese warlord of Manchuria. Their hopes then had been frustrated by the Tanaka government's refusal to follow up their action, but in 1931 they were to succeed in setting Japan upon a drastically different course.

On the night of 18 September 1931 a small explosion very slightly damaged the track of the South Manchurian Railway outside Mukden. Though undoubtedly engineered by Japanese officers, it was used as a pretext for driving the Chinese garrison from the town. In the following two months Foreign Minister Shidehara strove desperately to negotiate a settlement, but only a capitulation by the Chinese government to Japanese demands for Chinese troop withdrawal and Sino–Japanese negotiations could have satisfied the Japanese Army. By March 1932 Japanese forces had overrun the whole of Manchuria. Under the name of Manchukuo it was promoted to nominal nationhood by the Kwantung Army. Pu Yi, a survivor of the Manchu dynasty, was brought to Manchukuo, from which the dynasty had originally sprung, to become its emperor. In reality, however, every decision of the new state was taken by Japanese soldiers and advisers.

The 'Manchurian Incident' is often regarded as the first step towards the Second World War. China appealed to the League of Nations which rejected Japan's case, but its inability to enforce the judgement of the Lytton Commission revealed its impotence against an 'aggressor nation'. Japan's leaders argued that the League's standards could not be rigidly applied to Manchuria, and that there was no other recourse but force to defend their legitimate interests. When the League refused to modify its principles, Japan was faced with a choice between loss of face by withdrawal or military adventurism.

Between 1933 and 1936 the Army gained increasing control of Japanese foreign policy. Helped by divisions within Chiang K'ai-shek's Chinese Nationalist government, Japanese field commanders were able to protect Manchukuo by erecting buffer administrations in North China under accommodating, semi-independent Chinese generals. Russian interests in northern Manchuria were bought out, but large sums were spent on expanding and modernising the Army in anticipation of an imminent conflict with the Soviet Union. In 1934 the Foreign Ministry followed suit by warning other Powers against interference in Chinese affairs. Finally, in 1936 the Navy eventually had its way when the naval limitations agreements were abrogated by Japan and she was freed from all restrictions.

This drastic change of course isolated Japan in world affairs. Between 1931 and 1936 she was entirely without friends or allies, apart from the puppet government of Manchukuo. How was it that this situation, regarded as highly dangerous ever since the early Meiji period, was accepted by both public opinion and the non-military élites in Japan? For a more complete answer it is necessary to turn to economic and social developments.

The great depression which had begun in America in 1929 hit the Japanese people very hard. Japan's major export was silk. Ironically, though a luxury item, it was produced by peasants who needed the pittance paid for their toil to keep their income above starvation level. When the value of silk exports dropped by two-thirds, many small peasants were ruined, and some families were reduced to selling their daughters into prostitution in order to eat.

Already before 1930 peasant hardships had brought into existence tenant unions which agitated for better conditions. The Depression did not so much accentuate peasant discontent, however, as transform it. Tenants now turned their anger from the landlords towards the politicians and business leaders who appeared to be responsible for their fate. This response was typical also of many small businessmen who had been made bankrupt by the economic crisis, and whose plight compared strikingly with that of the large industrial combines, the *zaibatsu*, with their greater competitiveness and financial reserves.

The sight of a few growing richer as the vast majority were impoverished created a mood of deep dissatisfaction. Free international trade had previously been accepted as the best way for the country to increase its wealth and ensure that its now fast increasing population would be an asset rather than a liability. After 1930 many Japanese felt unable to rely solely on world markets, particularly when other nations placed special tariffs and quota restrictions on cheap Japanese exports.

As internationalism turned sour for many Japanese, Manchuria emerged as a promised land, which would absorb Japan's surplus rural population and reduce Japan's dependence on potentially hostile countries. It was against this background that the Army was able to make its successful incursion into foreign policy.

It was also the background for dramatic events within Japan. In 1931, the year after Hamaguchi's attempted assassination, secret conspiracies for the violent overthrow of civilian government hatched by army officers were only just warded off by their more conservative superiors. Then, in 1932, came a spate of plots and assassinations. In February the victims were the previous Finance Minister and the chief director of Mitsui, the largest *zaibatsu*. Then, on the fateful day of 15 May, Inukai Ki, the last pre-war Prime Minister of a party cabinet, was shot. Public sympathy for the assassins, mostly young officers, was such that they received very light sentences, and the Emperor's advisers felt it advisable to ride with the storm by appointing a retired admiral to head the next cabinet instead of a party leader.

These episodes were only the most striking examples of a series of terrorist actions by extreme nationalist groups. Particularly among the smallest of the 250-odd societies, the most active members saw themselves as the bearers of true *samurai* tradition—warriors whose duty it was to reject shabby compromise and cut down the self-seeking advisers who had misled the Emperor. Some even likened themselves to the loyalists of the Meiji Restoration years. Almost all the ultranationalists called for a Shōwa Restoration (*Shōwa*—Enlightenment and Harmony—being the ironically inappropriate reign-name chosen in 1926 for the present Emperor, Hirohito). What was meant by a Shōwa Restoration, however, varied widely.

The extreme nationalists were most united in their demand for a strong and decisive foreign policy, though even here there were differences. Some favoured crude military expansion, but others cherished the ideal of Pan–Asian solidarity under Japanese leadership. Another disagreement was between those who were preoccupied with Russia and security in the north and those who looked to expansion in South-East Asia. Such divisions ran right through the ultranationalist movement.

Much more important than these divisions were differences in basic philosophy. Several of the earlier and better supported ultranationalist societies, including some led by ministers or ex-ministers, were essentially

72

Prime Minister Hamaguchi is carried into hospital after ▶
being shot by a fanatical nationalist in 1930

conservative or reactionary, preaching a return to the traditional virtues of loyalty, obedience, and frugality. They believed passionately that Japan had a unique heritage of social harmony, which was threatened by liberal and Marxist notions of individualism, equality and social emancipation.

Such societies easily secured backing from wealthy business leaders. At the other end of the movement, however, there were groups which could best be described as National Socialist. Most were influenced by Kita Ikki, whose banned work *An Outline Proposal for the Reconstruction of Japan* advocated the abolition of the Diet, the confiscation of large fortunes and the mobilisation of Japan's resources against the Western Powers—the 'haves' who oppressed the 'have-nots'. Yet another section of the radical wing of ultranationalism was concerned primarily with the rural population. Inspired by such prophets as Gondō Seikyō, these groups believed in *Nōhonshugi*, the idea that the peasant should be treated as the foundation of the state. In its extreme form this concept had limited appeal, for the turning back to a pre-industrial past which Gondō advocated was utterly unrealistic and utopian. In its resentment against the big towns and the unequal distribution of the wealth resulting from modernisation, however, it gained enormous sympathy. It was a group attached to this section which murdered Inukai.

The rise of the ultranationalist movement reflected the difficulties and complexities which rapid modernisation had caused Japan. Like a barometer, it indicated the reaction felt by Japanese as they became conscious of the disruptive effects which the acceptance of Western ideas and practices could have on social harmony and national unity. When, in the early 1930s, foreign and domestic crises coincided and converged, the swing was a violent one towards the conviction that the price of belonging to the international community was too high.

Japanese now turned, influenced partly by fascist currents in Europe, towards the idea of a 'Revived Japan' with Tokugawa overtones. Western ideas could no longer be completely excluded, but 'dangerous thoughts' were clamped down on severely. Nor could Japan again be economically self-supporting; nevertheless, by controlling Manchuria and dominating China she could hope to build an East Asian bloc independent of the outside world. Like most attempts to gain total security, it was to prove an impossible dream.

11

The Triumph
of Militarism

The chief beneficiary of the swing towards traditionalism was the Army. Seven centuries of military rule had made it natural for Japanese to respect the soldier, and *bushidō* ideals had been inculcated into every Japanese schoolchild. Within the Army's ranks ability was all-important and birth of little account. In contrast to politicians and businessmen, the Army appeared to stand for integrity and the national good.

These advantages were brought to the fore by the Manchurian Incident. When large-scale military operations developed it was inevitable that the Army should have a major voice in foreign policy. Indeed, in the establishment of Manchukuo and the co-operative administrations in north China it was not merely the Army but local commanders who set the pace. Before long, however, the Army was to extend its influence to the whole of Japanese government.

This development was largely due to the special character of the Japanese Army. Like most organisations in Japan, it was plagued by factional divisions, based in part on regional rivalries. The long dominance of generals from Chōshū was coming to an end by 1930, and in 1932 the new Army Minister, General Araki, purged many senior Chōshū officers from influential posts, thereby inaugurating a bitter feud.

Araki's faction—the Kōdōha (Imperial Way Faction)—had another

The military insurgents of 26 February 1936, led by young officers,
occupy the Tōkyō Metropolitan Police Headquarters

rival, more formidable than the Chōshū clique. This was the Tōseiha
(Control Faction). Whereas the Kōdōha was traditionalist in approach,
placing great emphasis on morale and *bushidō* values, the Tōseiha was
more concerned with introducing to Japan the most up-to-date military
techniques such as tanks, air support, and the mobilisation of the whole
economy in preparation for war. This difference of emphasis had political
implications. The Kōdōha tended to sympathise with the common soldier
in his resentment against politics, big business and the cities. The Tōseiha,
on the other hand, was more interested in increasing industrial production
in order to secure greater military mechanisation. Rather than risk
bringing the economy to a halt, it was willing to co-operate with the
politicians, businessmen, and bureaucrats. Although it contained the
most able officers and was steadily gaining a monopoly of key planning
positions, however, the Tōseiha was not completely dominant in the
Army before 1936. Not the least of its difficulties was the jealousy of the
mass of officers who, unlike Tōseiha leaders, had been trained in the Military Academy without going on to the more prestigious War College.

These divisions came to a head at the beginning of 1936. On the night of

76

26 February, as the streets of Tōkyō lay buried under snow, about 1400 soldiers from the crack First Division and Imperial Guards seized key positions in the capital.

It was the bloodiest night in modern Japanese political history. Among those murdered were a recent Prime Minister, Admiral Saitō, the Finance Minister, the inspector-general of military education, and the existing Prime Minister's brother-in-law, who heroically misled the assassins about his identity. Others who narrowly escaped were Prince Saionji, and two senior imperial advisers, Count Makino and Admiral Suzuki.

The aim of the young officers who staged the mutiny was two-fold; to place the Kōdōha generals in charge of the Army and the government, and to rid Japan of corruption in high places. For three days senior officers wavered between suppression and concession. As the initial shock gradually wore off, however, authority re-asserted itself. The Tōseiha was determined not to let its rivals profit from the young officers' audacity, and it had a powerful ally in the Navy, which was prepared to land marines or bombard the rebels' position to maintain discipline.

The decision which sealed the mutiny's fate, however, was that of the Emperor. At some personal risk, he insisted on rejecting the rebels' claim that they were acting out of loyalty to him. When this was made known to the mutinous troops many deserted their leaders, leaving them no choice but surrender or death. Perhaps because the rebel officers hoped for the publicity of a show trial, only one committed *hara-kiri*.

Any such hopes were to be disappointed: the young officers had come too close to overthrowing the political system. A secret trial swiftly sentenced them to execution and several civilian ultranationalists suffered the same fate, among them Kita Ikki. General Mazaki, the most ambitious Kōdōha leader, was disgraced. The Tōseiha stood supreme.

To other Japanese it seemed less certain that order had been definitely restored. Their fears gave the Tōseiha a crucial weapon. It was easy, and plausible, to object now to any policies of which the Army disapproved on the grounds that these might cause uncontrollable unrest among radical officers. The political advantage this gave was soon evident. With the escalation of war against China in 1937 generals began to be appointed to head civilian ministries. Between 1937 and 1945 the Army even supplied four out of Japan's eight Prime Ministers.

In this new situation the Tōseiha found it much easier to gear Japan for total war, and in 1938 the Diet was induced to pass a National General

Mobilisation Law which gave the government potentially unlimited powers over industry. There had, in fact, already been a remarkable switch from light to heavy industry, as the markets for Japanese silk and textiles had contracted and government orders for munitions and equipment had grown. Despite this rapid recovery from the Depression, however, Japan's military planners were still worried by her lack of vital raw materials, notably oil, bauxite and rubber.

The Army also put its weight behind the campaign for spiritual mobilisation. This campaign had a strong traditionalist flavour. Its focus was the revival of Shintō myths of the divine descent of the Yamato dynasty, designed to surround the Emperor with even greater sanctity. In the name of *kokutai*, the uniquely Japanese form of imperial rule, liberal ideas followed Marxism and anarchism into the shadows. Scholars suffered persecution if they challenged the official version of Japan's unique racial and political heritage. Historians who lived through this period of military domination remember it as the 'dark valley'.

To ensure that the imperial ideology penetrated to the lowest levels the government turned to traditional methods of social organisation. From 1938 ward, hamlet and neighbourhood associations like those of Tokugawa times were imposed by the Home Ministry all over the country. Every citizen was forced to belong, and through them he was subjected to a barrage of propaganda. In enforcing conformity and checking dissent these associations played a crucial role.

Both contemporary observers and later writers have remarked upon the similarities between Japan in these years and the régimes of Hitler and Mussolini. In each there were rigid controls over economy and society, and the concept of class conflict was denied. Individualism was rejected in favour of the traditional idea of the family, and racial superiority was emphasised to an irrational degree. Violence and force were often idealised and humanitarianism frequently despised.

Despite these common characteristics, however, there were basic differences which make the term 'fascism' misleading if applied to Japan without qualification. In Japan the Emperor remained as a figurehead, and there was no real equivalent to the mass party which in Germany and Italy swept to power under a demagogic leader. Just as Japan had been less democratic, so in the 1930s she was less revolutionary. Instead of the overthrow of the old establishment, there was a shift, substantial, but not necessarily irreversible, in the balance of influence among the various

78

A teacher and his pupils take part in the celebration in 1937 of the supposed founding of the Japanese state by the first emperor, Jimmu, 2,597 years earlier—one of many occasions employed for instilling patriotic ardour in the late 1930s

élites. The Diet suffered an eclipse, but remained in existence. Most of the politicians' power was lost, but even the amalgamation of all parties into the Imperial Rule Assistance Association in 1940 did not destroy their separate identity. Twenty per cent of the successful candidates in the 1942 election had defeated official nominees. Much political power passed into the Army's hands, but even the Army was not supreme. The Japanese tradition of compromise and sectionalism was too strong to be pushed aside, even in time of war. As well as having to respect the wishes of the Navy, the Army depended upon the co-operation of the bureaucracy and the *zaibatsu*. Nor could it entirely ignore the Emperor's close advisers, men who generally were cautious conservatives. All these provided checks upon totalitarianism—one of the most important ingredients of fascism.

Rather than fascism, therefore, it would be more accurate to speak of two main trends, militarism and the revival of conservative authoritarianism, both connected and both having traditionalist as well as fascist overtones. As so often in modern Japanese history, modern and traditional went hand in hand. This time, however, the combination was to lead to disaster.

79

12

The Pacific War

Though the triumph of militarism undoubtedly brought war nearer, it did not make it inevitable. Few Japanese wanted it, even within the Army and Navy. Ironically, it was the pursuit of total security which finally brought catastrophe to Japan.

Japan's real difficulties only began when Europe plunged into war. Before 1939–40 her efforts to construct a 'New Order' in East Asia had brought blame and recrimination but no counter-measures. None of the Powers was prepared to support China by force, even after July 1937, when, following a minor clash and an initial mishandling, full-scale hostilities broke out between Japan and China.

The 'China Incident' as this war was inaptly called in Japan, was a tragic accident. As in the past, Japan's leaders failed to understand why China would not accept her view of East Asian co-operation, while on the Chinese side the course of the war soon showed that the Japanese military machine had become more formidable than Chiang K'ai-shek and some of his generals had bargained for.

It was formidable, also, in a more ominous way. The brutality with which Nanking, the Chinese Nationalist capital, was treated when captured by the Japanese has few parallels. In scale it exceeded the episodes of cruelty which other nations were soon to suffer from Japan.

The contrast between such behaviour and the gentleness and warmth displayed by ordinary Japanese in their home life demands explanation. In *The Chrysanthemum and the Sword*, a work written during the Pacific War, the distinguished American anthropologist, Ruth Benedict, argued persuasively that the key lay in Japan's system of situational ethics. Whereas in Western societies basic values were universally applicable to all men, in Japan they varied in accordance with particular group relationships and hierarchical status. In dealing with foreigners there were no definite rules. When relations with them were hostile, therefore, there would be no checks on Japanese behaviour.

It is also argued that in any hierarchical society the lowest ranking will tend to channel their frustrations into aggression against outsiders. In Japan's case those frustrations were great, particularly among recruits who had suffered poverty and hardship as peasants and were now brutally bullied by older soldiers. One should remember that Japanese troops were fighting in difficult conditions, outnumbered by their enemies and short of food and medical supplies, and that Allied prisoners who surrendered were acting in a way which Japanese soldiers were taught to despise.

Despite the numerical odds against them, the Japanese made striking advances into central China and along the coast after July 1937. Nevertheless, both Chinese Nationalists and Communists resisted stubbornly and it was obvious that Japan could not successfully occupy the whole of China. Japanese Army Headquarters had actually been less eager to turn hostilities into all-out war than had Prime Minister Konoe. After Konoe's resignation in January 1939, therefore, a new attempt at a settlement with Chiang K'ai-shek aimed at economic co-operation and joint action against Mao Tse-tung's troublesome Communists was not a complete impossibility. Once again, however, events in Europe intervened.

The outbreak of war in Europe in September 1939 seemed to present Japan with a golden opportunity for an easy settlement of the Chinese question, with the additional possibility of excluding European influence from South-East Asia. By capitalising on French and British weakness it was hoped to cut Chiang K'ai-shek off from the supply routes which had been aiding Chinese resistance. In June 1940 Japan forced France to close the border between Tongking and China and in September made her first demand for the stationing of troops along French Indo-China's frontier with China. During the following year her requirements steadily increased

THE PACIFIC WAR [see overleaf]

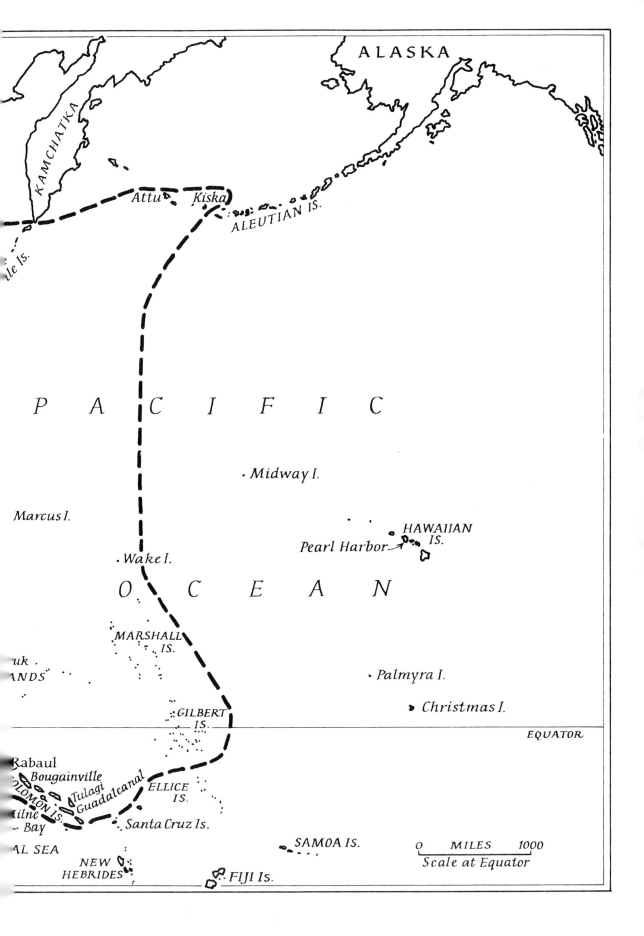

until she came close to occupying the whole colony. Britain, too, found it expedient to submit to Japanese pressure for the closure of the Burma Road between July and October 1940, when the war in Europe was critical.

At the same time as it opened the way in South-East Asia, the war in Europe gave Japan greater security in the north. Relations with Russia had been generally strained. Russia was known to be encouraging Chiang K'ai-shek against Japan, and the ill-defined boundaries of Manchukuo offered abundant scope for border clashes. In 1938 there was a serious clash on the Korean border and in 1939 the battle of Nomonhan on the Manchukuo border facing Outer Mongolia raged all summer, with Japanese forces receiving a sound hammering from Russia's superior tank divisions. After 1939, however, Stalin had to pay more attention to Hitler's ambitions and was happy in April 1941 to sign a non-aggression treaty with Japan.

Unfortunately for Japan, the war in Europe also had a major effect on American attitudes. The Roosevelt Administration had previously shown great concern about Japanese aggression and infringement of American economic interests in China, but even when the USS *Panay* was deliberately strafed and sunk by Japanese planes in Chinese waters there was no attempt at retaliation. Whatever they might have wished, American governments were fettered by the strong tide of isolationism in public opinion. Hitler's dramatic conquests, however, caused a marked change, and in July 1940, after Japan's first advance into South-East Asia, Washington placed an embargo on the export of certain strategic materials.

From this point on the chain of events led directly towards war. On 27 September 1940 the Japanese government, again under Konoe's leadership, after much hesitation signed a defensive alliance with Germany and Italy. Foreign Minister Matsuoka, who with the Army was chiefly responsible for this Tripartite Pact, claimed that it would deter America from interfering with the signatories' designs for erecting large spheres of influence. It was the fears of the Emperor and the Navy, however, which proved more accurate. Instead of being intimidated, Washington now became convinced that there were much closer links between the aggressor nations than actually existed and that it was essential to make a firm stand against the 'fascist conspiracy'.

During the first half of 1941 Japan and America both sought security without fully understanding the other's position. As Japan made further diplomatic and military advances towards the raw materials of South-East

84

Asia, America, in collaboration with Britain and Holland, imposed further sanctions, culminating in the freezing of Japanese assets and trade by the three countries on 26 July 1941. This action amounted to a diplomatic time-bomb. Japan held less than two years' reserve of oil. Without replenishment she would eventually be helpless in the face of an American threat. Unless she was to abandon all her gains of the last ten years, therefore, she must steel herself to challenge her mighty adversary forthwith.

There remained one possible way out of this agonising dilemma—a diplomatic settlement. By mid-1941 the stiffening of America's attitude had caused deep concern even among military circles, and Konoe and other civilian leaders now grasped at the new possibility of realistic negotiation. The talks which Ambassador Nomura had been conducting in Washington with Secretary of State Cordell Hull since February assumed the highest priority, and Japan seriously considered withdrawing from South-East Asia and ending the war with China.

All was to no avail. Japan's actions had aroused such suspicion that America now required complete withdrawal from China and guarantees of future good conduct. When, therefore, Japan's suggestion of a summit meeting between Prince Konoe and President Roosevelt to cut the knot of mistrust was rejected, an imperial conference decided on 6 September 1941 to go to war in October if the negotiations had not succeeded.

No progress had been achieved by 12 October, the deadline date. Still, however, Konoe hoped for a settlement. He knew that the Navy secretly supported his willingness to make greater concessions if they would prevent war. The Navy was not prepared to make a stand, however, and in the face of the strong line taken by the Army Minister, Tōjō Hideki, Konoe was left with no option but to resign.

Konoe's successor was a surprise choice—Tōjō, the very minister who had caused the previous cabinet's resignation. He was a Tōseiha general with little political experience but a reputation for discipline. It was felt that as head of the government he might adopt a more responsible attitude and at the same time keep the Army under control. He was specifically instructed by the Emperor not to take the decision for war as binding and to continue negotiations with America. But on 26 November Cordell Hull flatly rejected Japan's new proposals and refused to budge from his initial position. Acceptance of his terms would have meant great humiliation to Japan and by totally discrediting Japan's leadership and revealing the bankruptcy of the policies pursued at great cost over several years might

An episode from one of the most daring and most carefully planned military operations in history. An aerial photograph taken during the attack on the American Pacific fleet at Pearl Harbor

well have endangered the whole 'emperor system'. On 1 December 1941 the final decision for war was made in Tōkyō.

Both countries had gambled, but only Japan had understood the magnitude of the gamble. America was made aware of it on the morning of 7 December when, before war had actually been declared, a Japanese seaborne bomber force knocked out much of the American Pacific fleet at its Hawaian base. The Pearl Harbor attack was the prelude to one of the most rapid and extraordinary conquests ever known. To offset America's superior potential it was vital for Japan to gain speedy control of the resources of South-East Asia, particularly the Dutch East Indies, and to hold a strategic perimeter of islands in the Pacific in order to make counter-attack difficult. If America then decided that her Asian interests did not justify the effort and expense of a long and bitter campaign, Japan's gamble would have succeeded.

By mid-1942 the main Japanese aims had been achieved. The British colonies of Burma and Malaya, the supposedly impregnable Singapore, the Dutch East Indies, and the Philippines had all fallen, while Indo-China and Thailand were subservient satellites. Most of the Pacific island chains were in Japanese hands. Yet already the tide was beginning to turn. Pearl Harbor had united the American people and their determination to secure revenge was shown in the increase in American production of war materials. In May 1942, in the Battle of the Coral Sea, the Japanese Navy suffered losses it could ill afford. In June the Battle of Midway saw the first defeat of a Japanese fleet. The long drawn-out struggle for Guadalcanal during the 1942–3 winter marked the first step in the Allied recovery of territory occupied by Japan. From this time on the story was essentially one of American power with British Empire and Australasian support against Japanese courage, symbolised by the *kamikaze* pilots who flew many terrifying suicide missions against American warships.

The final outcome of the struggle could hardly be in doubt even though the true facts of the war were hidden from the Japanese people and sometimes even from Tōjō. Japan's war effort suffered from fundamental

The end of a *kamikaze* fighter. An American warship narrowly escapes the attack of a Japanese Zero plane. When normal fighting methods proved helpless to resist Allied advances in the latter stages of the Pacific War many Japanese pilots attempted to destroy an enemy ship by diving headlong at it. Some were successful

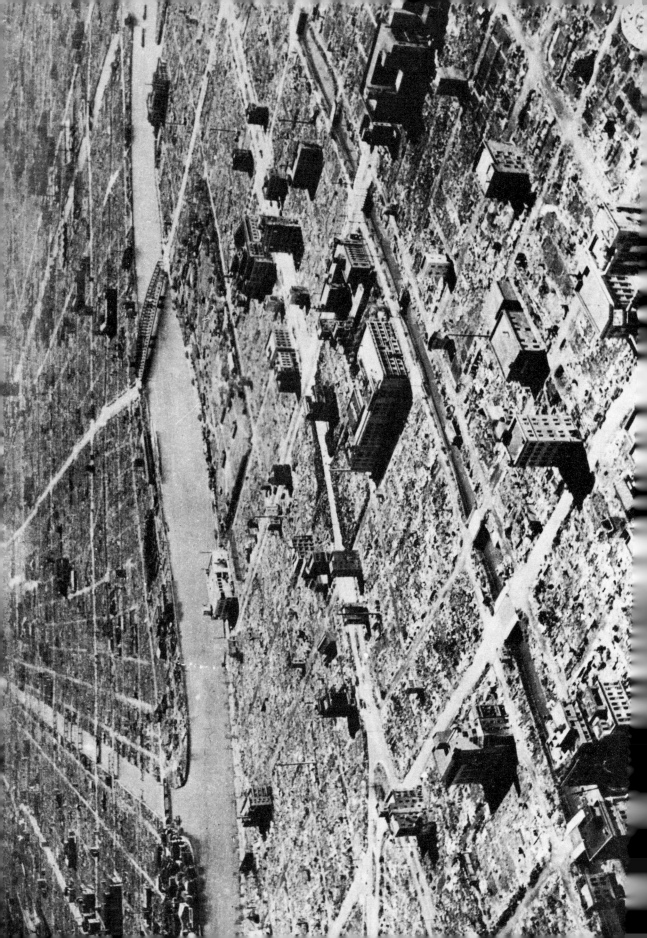

weaknesses. Some were due to the nature of Japanese society. It was not uncommon for the Army to conscript workers engaged in vital production for the Navy, or vice versa, and towards the end of the war the Army even built some submarines which it needed because it could not rely on naval co-operation! There was, however, a much more serious deficiency than the factionalism and sectionalism which undermined Japanese planning. This was the shortage of shipping. If Japan was to make use of the resources she had acquired she would have to be able to transport them to Japan. Yet so devastating were American submarines that by mid-1945 Japan had less than a tenth of the ocean-going merchant ships she had in 1941.

On the home front the Japanese people suffered great hardship from the unequal war into which they had been led. After an initial wave of exuberance following the casting-off of Japan's lingering sense of inferiority towards the West, Japanese found themselves forced to put up with increasing material shortages, and their situation was often little better than that existing in Japanese prisoner-of-war camps. It was impossible to import much of the Korean rice on which the Japanese people depended to keep their calorie intake above subsistence level, and cuts in fertiliser imports lowered Japan's own production. Though the rationing system was moderately effective, townspeople were much worse off than peasants. By 1945 nearly a million people were regularly making Sunday expeditions out of Tōkyō to barter their valuables for vegetables and fruit.

Despite their worsening plight there were no mutterings of opposition to the war among the Japanese. Apart from their traditional habit of obedience to authority and the tight social organisation, they were inundated with war propaganda. One of the major themes was the Great East Asia Co-Prosperity Sphere, which successfully combined a natural gratification at Japan's military exploits with the traditional idea of Japan aiding her Asian brothers to liberate themselves from Western imperialism.

The reality was more sordid. As essential elements in Japan's war effort, the colonies which Japan had taken over from her opponents were exploited even more ruthlessly than they had been before. The granting of independence came only when defeat was in sight. Nevertheless, by discrediting the West, Japan made an important, if negative, contribution to the post-war movement for colonial emancipation.

The worst sufferings of the Japanese people came in the last nine months of the war. From November 1944 incendiary bombs began to rain almost nightly on cities largely made up of wooden buildings. Large districts were

89

◀ Tōkyō suffered devastation from bombing raids in the last nine months of the war. This is central Tōkyō in August 1945 reduced to ashes. After one raid in March 1945 when a high wind fanned the flames, it was estimated that 197,000 were dead or missing in Tōkyō. Loss of life was so great that mass evacuation began, and more than three million left Tōkyō alone in 1945.

Accustomed as they were to devastating air-raids, few Japanese outside Hiroshima and Nagasaki paid much attention to the news of two air attacks on these cities on 6 and 9 August respectively, and fewer still realised that Japan had become the first victim of nuclear attack. The American decision to drop atom bombs on Japan is .hard to justify. Although it was officially claimed that it was the only way of avoiding an invasion of Japan which would have cost many thousands of lives, the Truman Administration was by this time well aware that the Japanese government was anxious to make peace. Tōjō had been replaced in July 1944, and a secret peace party had come into being, with support from several elder statesmen, including Prince Konoe. It was known to the US government that an approach had been made to Russia, in the vain hope of securing Stalin's mediation. One thing only held the cabinet of Suzuki Kantarō back from replying positively to the Allies' Potsdam Declaration of 26 July 1945, which vaguely threatened 'utter destruction' if Japan did not accept unconditional surrender—the fear that the Emperor would be deposed. If America could have accepted this one condition, surrender might not have been long delayed, the Army's reluctance notwithstanding.

Ironically, it is far from certain that the dropping of atom bombs really did decide Japan to surrender. Although the Emperor was deeply moved by the nuclear destruction, another development which occurred on 8 August 1945 may well have had a greater immediate effect. This was Russia's entry into the war against Japan and swift advance through Manchukuo. The possibility of a Communist takeover compelled Japan's leaders to act swiftly. On 9 August an imperial conference was called. The Army still wanted to hold out for certain conditions and the debate lasted into the night, but with the most important members of the government equally divided the Emperor was in a position to assert his own will for once and he cast his decision in favour of surrender. Even then the drama was not ended, for another conference had to be held on 14 August, when America refused to guarantee the Emperor's position. Once again the Emperor placed Japan's need for peace above personal considerations. The struggle which had caused the death of more than three million Japanese and made at least ten million homeless was at an end.

13

Japan
under Occupation

Japan officially surrendered on 2 September 1945. In a radio broadcast announcing Japan's defeat the Emperor had stated that the Japanese people must now 'endure the unendurable'. Having been swamped with propaganda assuring them that the Japanese spirit would triumph over American material superiority, the Japanese now had to adjust to the fact of defeat and occupation. Nor was this to be any occupation of the traditional kind, for the American government, working through the Supreme Commander of the Allied Powers in Japan, General MacArthur, set itself the task of creating a new Japan, peaceful and democratic instead of militaristic and reactionary.

On the face of it, the idea of a young, if powerful, state attempting to refashion the basic patterns of a country with five times as long a historical background and a very different culture seemed incredibly ambitious and optimistic. Yet there were powerful factors at work on America's side.

The most important factor was the Japanese response. Although some officers committed *hara-kiri* rather than suffer the shame of surrender, American fears of a hostile reaction among the population at large were confounded. There were many reasons for this passive, and fairly soon favourable, response, ranging from resigned acceptance of the inevitable and disillusionment with Japan's previous ideals to positive sympathy with American intentions. Before the 'dark valley', after all, there had been many intellectuals, politicians, and businessmen who had admired aspects of the West. What the Occupation proposed found a foundation in the democratic tendencies, limited though they were, of Taishō Japan.

The second major factor aiding the fulfilment of American aims was the authority concentrated in the hands of MacArthur. Japanese often spoke of him as a new *shōgun*. Although in theory the Occupation was an Allied one, in reality it was predominantly an American affair, which the American government left largely in MacArthur's hands, once it had laid down an initial basic policy. Other Allies actually had less scope for altering or toning down the Occupation programme than the Japanese themselves, for America had promised to give full expression to the people's wishes, and MacArthur could not govern directly because of language difficulties but had to work through the Japanese bureaucracy. Nevertheless, in the last resort MacArthur had the rights of a conqueror, and on many occasions he did not hesitate to use them.

The basic objective of the Occupation was to ensure that Japan never again threatened world peace. It sought to achieve this by two means—demilitarisation and democratisation. Demilitarisation was much the easier target. Militarism was so discredited that there was no outcry against the complete abolition of Japan's armed forces. The Occupation authorities even wrote into Japan's new constitution an article renouncing forever the use of military force in international affairs. It was an extreme measure, extraordinarily idealistic, but one which gave Japan a uniquely pacifist status and undoubtedly appealed to many war-weary Japanese.

Democratisation was a much more complex matter, rendered all the more difficult because the Occupation authorities did not know how much time they had and were therefore forced to work at speed. Not all their 'experts' were well-informed about Japanese conditions and some of their reforms were half-baked attempts to impose American practices in un-modified form. Nevertheless, a number of much-needed changes were carried out.

The change which had the greatest effect was the Land Reform of 1946. This measure solved at one stroke the major social injustice of pre-war years—the tenant problem. Its almost revolutionary character was partly accidental, however. The Occupation sought to end large and absentee landlordship by limiting holdings to seven and a half acres. The state would buy the rest and sell it to the former tenants at a reasonable price

92

'The new *shōgun* and the old figurehead': General MacArthur and Emperor ▶
Hirohito in 1945. The Japanese government attempted to suppress this
photograph because it considered it disrespectful

over a long period. What actually happened was that after prices had been fixed, rapid inflation set in. Peasants found themselves in the happy position of being able to buy long-desired land for the price of a few cigarettes.

This was not the only Occupation attempt to assist the underprivileged. Trade unions had always suffered from repression in pre-war Japan. Their membership had never reached half a million, and during the Pacific War they had all been dissolved. MacArthur's Labor Section regarded unions as a vital support of political democracy. So successful was its encouragement that by 1949 union membership had grown to more than six million.

Reform of the *zaibatsu* was also projected, but ran up against subtle opposition. It was curtailed about 1948, when reforming ardour was being forced to take second place to economic recovery. Japan had lost a vast amount of industrial plant from American bombing and after the war she had no empire to ease her lot. Not only was she deprived of Manchuria, Korea and Taiwan, but even some islands to which she had a strong traditional claim. Because of the general uncertainty, moreover, industrialists in Japan were hesitant to build up their enterprises. All this meant that America was forced to send aid to Japan instead of being able to make Japan repay with her own resources the countries she had invaded.

Economic reforms were matched on the social side. Education was made more open by the erection of a basically comprehensive three-tiered schools system, topped by a large number of colleges and universities. This American-style scheme undoubtedly imposed great strains and has been generally condemned in Japan for causing a dilution in quality by over-stretching Japanese financial and teaching resources. It was accompanied however, by other, less criticised, attempts at liberalisation. Women were given equal rights, and restrictions on press freedom removed. To confirm the break with the past, official support of Shintō was ended, and the Emperor announced in a New Year's Day broadcast that he was not divine.

For the economic and social reforms to play their part in supporting democracy, a new political system needed to be established. Many Japanese felt that the Meiji Constitution could still provide the best framework, but the Occupation authorities insisted on a clear formulation of popular sovereignty. Eventually they grew impatient at Japanese prevarication and drafted their own constitution. Translated into slightly awkward Japanese, it was pushed through the Diet in 1946 and remains in force today. The Emperor's functions were reduced to rubber-stamping the decisions of the Diet, now explicitly declared the highest organ of government and consisting of two houses, both elected, but with the House of Representatives much more important than the House of Councillors. Cabinets are responsible only to the Diet, but legislation is subject to judicial review to ensure that it abides by the constitution. The constitution itself can only be changed by a two-thirds majority of both houses of the Diet. The final major feature is an extensive bill of rights, giving protection for almost every conceivable freedom.

While the Occupation lasted it could not be entirely foreseen what the effects of all these changes would be on politics. There was some evidence, however, that despite the flurry of activity, Japanese government would not be entirely different from before. A Socialist party had made a swift rise, flanked by a much smaller Communist movement, but after a brief and unhappy experience as chief partner in a coalition cabinet in 1947–8, the former's prospects began to look less bright. It was a conservative ex-diplomat, Yoshida Shigeru, who emerged as the dominant figure, enjoying American confidence at the same time as he won popular support for his more independent attitude towards the Occupation authorities. Yoshida's success, however, owed much to the Occupation purge of Japanese deemed guilty of war responsibility. Among the 220,000 removed from positions of influence were many senior politicians. What would happen if they attempted to regain their previous standing when the Occupation ended was anyone's guess. In fact, none were to make more than brief comebacks, but their resentment of Yoshida was to play a considerable part in forcing him out of office in 1954.

The political future would have been even more uncertain had there not been a fundamental shift of emphasis in Occupation policy during 1947–8. By this stage the extreme efforts towards democratisation were bringing results which were not altogether pleasing to MacArthur. The ending of the emperor system had left an ideological vacuum of which Marxism found it easier than liberalism to take advantage. Some of the unions which had been newly formed seemed to be turning into irresponsible monsters, constantly calling strikes when Japan urgently needed an economic recovery. On top of this, the now highly decentralised police were completely unable to deal with the gangs and black marketeers whom Japan's economic dislocation was breeding.

The chief reason for reconsideration of Occupation policy, however, lay outside Japan. By 1948 the Communist takeover of China was imminent and the 'Cold War' had already commenced. In these circumstances the idea of a weak, neutral Japan was no longer just a luxury, but a real danger. America now needed an ally in East Asia, and she could not risk Japan's potential industrial power passing into Communist hands. Economic recovery now became the watchword. In its name some unions were prohibited from striking, and restrictions were later placed on Communist activity. The change naturally benefited the conservative political parties who looked to business for financial support. The Socialists, who had earlier supported Occupation changes, now became increasingly anti-American. They were further alienated when their idealistic concept of a pacifist Japan was infringed by American encouragement in 1950 of a 75,000-strong 'Police Reserve'—in actual fact, the nucleus of an unconstitutional army. The revised American policy was brought to its culmination with the ratification of a Japanese–American Security Treaty, which permitted numerous American bases in Japan and gave American forces very considerable freedom of action, on 28 April 1952, the same day on which the Occupation came to an end.

Perhaps the most important legacy of the Occupation was the balance it achieved, partly by accident, between encouragement of democracy and recovery of stability. The early reforms created the conditions for an active Socialist movement, while the relaxation of punitive measures against business provided backing for a powerful, but moderate, conservative force. Similarly, encouragement of 'grass roots' participation in politics and local government was unintentionally matched by American dependence on the bureaucracy, a powerful stabilising force. Much the same was true of social change. Almost all artificial restraints were removed, but there was not enough time to push individualism so far that it seriously threatened established social patterns.

No judgement on the Occupation can, as yet, be final. Future historians may well see it, however, as resembling the Taika Reform and the Meiji Restoration—a necessary revolution from above which introduced a new wave of foreign influence and paved the way for a fresh unleashing of Japan's human energy. It was, in one sense, fortunate for Japan that this revolution came from outside as well as from above and thus left no legacy of hatred and division within Japan.

14

Contemporary Japan

For almost a decade after the end of the American Occupation Japan's prospects did not look particularly bright. Her bid for empire had left a legacy of bitterness and suspicion overseas, while by the terms of the 1952 security treaty Japan was little more than an American satellite. Most economists were pessimistic about Japan's ability to support a growing population, and there were grave doubts as to whether democratic institutions would really take root.

Today most of these forebodings seem to have been left behind. One factor above all underlies the change of mood—Japan's 'economic miracle'. Since the early 1950s Japan has enjoyed an astonishing average annual growth rate of over ten per cent. With a gross national product of £69,344,583,458 at the end of 1969, she now stands as the world's third economic power. Living standards are not yet as high as those of most parts of Western Europe, let alone America, but affluence is in sight.

What is the explanation of Japan's unparalleled growth? The factor most often cited abroad is loyalty to one's employer. Once an employee joins a company, he rarely leaves it. Not only is his pay geared to length of service, but the company generally provides housing and holidays, and quite frequently even arranges employees' marriages. The same group mentality is reflected in the structure of unions which normally cover all

97

the workers in one particular enterprise. The general notion of working-class solidarity is clearly weaker than the sense of, and desire for, membership in a hierarchical group.

The other major tradition which has played a crucial role in Japan's economic expansion is that of élite control. Apart from the high level of government research and planning, there is a striking degree of influence by large banks. Japan presents the unusual spectacle of a country in which bank loans form more than two-thirds of the average company's capital resources. The banks themselves conduct a great deal of research into international conditions and long-term trends, and through the Bank of Japan are open to influence from the government. What they advise is therefore not only difficult to refuse but based on expert knowledge.

This research and guidance from above has played a large part in changing the pattern of Japanese industry. In the mid-1950s Japan was concentrating on the production of goods for which world demand was low. By the end of the 1960s a remarkable shift into heavy or sophisticated industry had taken place. With ships, steel, cameras, sewing-machines, watches, plastics, chemicals, motor-vehicles, and electronic equipment leading the way—nearly twenty-four million transistor radios were exported in 1967 alone, while in 1969 production of colour televisions had reached almost five million and tape recorders over eighteen million— exports have increased in some years by more than twenty per cent. Behind the scenes has been a labour force which has little time for demarcation disputes and is prepared to adjust to new tasks and learn new skills.

The adaptability and intelligence of Japan's workers are related to the high value which is attached to education. This, too, is rooted in tradition. It is also, however, connected with the unusual form of meritocracy practised in Japan. No firm of any size will recruit executives who have not been to university, and top companies confine themselves to the graduates of the major seats of learning, such as Tōkyō University. Competition to enter the leading universities is intense. Many students, known popularly as *rōnin*, make several attempts. University entrance, however, is only the last of several major hurdles. At each level of the education system, parents strive to secure entry for their children into the schools known to produce good results. Indeed, it is not uncommon for parents to move to a favoured district or send a child to live with relatives who are near good schools. The resulting pressure is a major social problem in Japan.

What makes Japanese meritocracy unusual is that after companies have

99

◄ The Yokosuke Thermal Power Station, south of Tōkyō. A typical example of the heavy industry clustered along the east coast belt, often on land reclaimed from the sea, which has made Japan the third largest economic power in the world but has also caused a massive pollution problem

Protesters against cases of death and illness from mercury poisoning, caused by industrial waste at Minamata, confront security guards of the corporation concerned and riot police

selected their graduates, ability has to take second place behind group harmony and security. It is rare for an executive to gain promotion out of line with his fellow entrants. From a Western viewpoint this ought to lead to inefficiency and lethargy. Clearly, however, in Japan it has been more than countered by company loyalty and group decision-making.

Not all the ingredients of economic success have had traditional overtones. By means of some 5,000 licence agreements Japan has bought the most up-to-date inventions of American and European technology, while quota restrictions and high tariffs have protected her domestic producers from foreign competition. In addition, freedom from responsibilities overseas and reliance on the American 'nuclear umbrella' for her protection has led to very light spending on defence. Moreover the Japanese economy has benefited enormously from supplying the American forces in Japan and the American war efforts in Korea and Vietnam.

Finally, the results of the Land Reform have been sensational. Before the war Japan imported one-fifth of her rice. Now, by increased use of fertilisers, the development of new strains of rice, and by the help of co-operatively owned machinery, she regularly produces a surplus—even though the proportion of the population engaged in agriculture has been halved to eighteen per cent, most of which is female.

It would be wrong to paint Japan's economic picture entirely in bright colours. Countries which have experienced very rapid industrialisation often face special difficulties, and Japan is no exception. The greatest current problem is pollution. The discharge of chemical waste into air and sea has exacted a heavy toll on life and health. While economic growth was the sole priority, moreover, expenditure on social welfare, housing, and proper sewage systems was kept to a minimum. No one who has tried to walk past a dung-collecting lorry on one of Tōkyō's many unpavemented streets could regard it as an ideal modern city, and it remains to be seen whether a halt can be called to the deterioration of the environment. Whether the genuine public concern now evident can make itself felt will be a real test of Japan's democratic institutions.

Pollution is a relatively new danger. Ever since the start of Meiji industrialisation, however, there has been a gulf between efficient large-scale industry and smaller enterprises, generally of a traditional kind, with low productivity. Workers in factories employing more than 500 are distinctly better off than those in smaller factories, while the great number in small workshops are even worse off, despite recent improvements.

Another old problem is Japan's dependence on world trade. Japan is still heavily dependent on other countries for certain crucial materials, notably oil and iron, and raw materials account for seventy per cent of her total imports. However, Japan's foreign trade takes up a considerably smaller proportion of her gross national product than Britain's, for example, and it would take a major world trade crisis to seriously threaten Japan's economic prosperity. Currently, indeed, Japan is embarrassed by a huge balance of payments surplus, built up largely at U.S. expense. Like President Nixon's shock decision in 1971 to visit Peking this has strained Japanese–American relations. However, since Prime Minister Satō's replacement by Tanaka Kakuei in July 1972 Japan has established diplomatic relations with Communist China and Japanese are increasingly optimistic about the possibility of reducing their dependence on America and achieving cooperation with China and Russia.

Notwithstanding her remaining difficulties, Japan's economic success is undisputed, a matter of great national pride. Politically it has brought great credit to the Liberal Democratic Party, which has governed Japan uninterruptedly since its formation out of the two major conservative parties in 1955. Other reasons can be found for the conservative domination of politics since 1948: traditional respect for authority, peasant support (the domestic price of rice is kept artificially high by the government), and financial backing from industry. Nevertheless, it is probably its successful management of the economy which has enabled the LDP to ride out with no great damage the few storms which have threatened its control.

Among these storms only one deserves to be termed a major crisis. It blew up in 1960, when the Kishi cabinet negotiated a revision of the Japanese–American Security Pact. Since Japan was conceded a greater degree of control over the use of American bases, the opposition to the revised treaty appeared at first sight unreasonable. Kishi's action, however, gave a focus to many of the deep fears about Japan's position and future felt by ordinary Japanese. Though the leadership of the opposition movement was taken by the left-wing parties, the militant students and the large and influential intellectual class, there was much support from those who feared direct involvement in the 'Cold War' or were concerned about a revival of militarism. The fact that Kishi was once a member of Tōjō's wartime cabinet, together with the knowledge that the LDP wished to revise the constitution, notably by removing the clause renouncing the use of war, gave some substance to the intellectuals' claim that this might be the first step on the road to the extinction of Japan's democratic system.

The protest against treaty revision reached its climax in a series of mass demonstrations in Tōkyō in June 1960. The proposed visit of President Eisenhower had to be cancelled, and after the treaty had passed through the Diet, Kishi, who had lost support within his party, was forced to resign. The opposition forces had clearly scored a partial victory. Yet in the election at the end of 1960 the LDP was returned with its customary resounding majority.

Nothing else has come so close to disturbing Japan's exceptional political stability. In 1969 the agitation for university reform made striking headlines as police and students fought pitched battles, and extremists created turmoil in higher education, but it gained much less public support. Not only did Prime Minister Sato (Kishi's brother) survive, but in the election in December 1969, the gradual trend towards a decline in the LDP's massive majority was actually reversed.

Despite the electoral success of the conservatives it is doubtful whether Japanese voters feel an emotional commitment to the LDP, and party membership is small. Moreover the party itself is really a coalition of nine or ten factions, which are virtually parties within a party and sometimes run rival candidates at elections. Each has a separate organisation and its own sources of funds. Most business groups and companies, in fact, make most of their indispensable financial contribution to politics through faction leaders with whom they have developed close ties.

Factional strength makes a conservative Prime Minister's life more precarious than it might appear to casual observers. There is always the possibility of a rival leader within the party winning the support of the factions for a change. This is much more likely than a swing to the opposition, for the latter is weak and fragmented. Plagued, like the conservatives, by factionalism, but with the added complication of ideological dissension based on a Marxist intellectual background, the Socialists have ceased to make headway. In the 1969 election they won only ninety seats, compared with the LDP's 300 and their own previous 134. The more moderate Democratic Socialists, who broke away from the main Socialist party in 1959, have even less mass appeal, and only 31 seats. The Communists recovered in the 1969 election to win fourteen seats, but, like other left-wing parties, no longer seem able to arouse enthusiasm among the young.

By European standards a hard core of support for the Left should have been provided by the growing urban proletariat, but this has largely been captured by a party which did not even exist in the 1950s. The Kōmeitō, which in 1969 became the third largest group in the Diet with forty-seven seats, is the political arm of the Sōka Gakkai, an offshoot of the Nichiren sect of Buddhism which claimed thirteen and a half million members in 1967. Its appeal seems to lie chiefly in its tight organisation, which offers a firm sense of belonging to the under-privileged or those who have just moved from the countryside to the cities.

The success of Sōka Gakkai has been repeated, on a less phenomenal scale, by several other new religions. Most of them have roots in Buddhism or Shintō, but combine them with other, more modern, influences, including the personalities of their remarkable founders. Their rise has not, however, led to the extinction of older sects. Traditional varieties of Buddhism still have almost sixty million registered followers while Shintō sects are supported by as many as sixty-five millions. Since Japan's total population in 1970 was 103,720,060, many Japanese clearly still see no reason to be as exclusively selective as Westerners in religious matters.

The appearance of numerous 'new religions' has given rise to the impression among some foreigners that post-war Japan has been engaged in the frantic pursuit of a new ideology to replace the discredited pre-war myths. This may be partly true, but it conceals the fact that for most Japanese ideology is less important than belonging to a clearly defined group. This basic need has been satisfied in most cases, not by new religions, but by company, student group, or family.

It also conceals the fact that those who have sought ideological certainty have found it in diverse ways. The Japanese who have turned to religion have been far outnumbered by those who have been strongly influenced, in their youth at any rate, by Marxism. Among teachers and intellectuals Marxist influence has been particularly strong. Other creeds and tendencies fashionable in America or Europe have enjoyed lesser vogues. But against these one should balance the number of Japanese who have been content to cultivate aspects of their own tradition, such as Nō drama, calligraphy, or the tea ceremony; who have found satisfaction in Western music (a large number of cafés exist where Japanese go to listen to classical records as much as to drink coffee); or whose leisure time is taken up by sport, whether it be watching traditional *sumō* wrestling or semi-traditional baseball, or engaging in newer sports like mountaineering, skiing or golf.

This diversity of ideology and attitude is hardly surprising in view of the great variety of choice in contemporary Japan. At the school level the Japanese child learns a good deal about both East and West and has inculcated in him values deriving from Western liberalism as well as Japan's own tradition, and, unofficially, Marxism. In the mass media the range of influences is no less wide. Television alone offers a bewildering variety, with several commercial channels as well as a close equivalent of the BBC. There is a vast number of magazines catering for every interest, including half a dozen monthly journals which provide a detailed coverage of current affairs and which reach a wide readership. It is significant, too, that the *Asahi Shimbun*, which is perhaps the most distinguished of Japan's newspapers, also has the highest circulation, selling altogether more than nine million copies of its morning and evening editions. Finally it should be mentioned that books in Japan are relatively cheap and the number of secondhand bookshops is a perennial object of envy to foreign scholars.

All this adds up to an open society, and the fact that the Japanese have mostly found it workable suggests that they have finally come to terms with modernisation. It is true that a few ultranationalists of the pre-war traditionalist, anti-Communist variety remain, and also that fears that post-war Japan has been throwing away a heritage which cannot be recreated,

Anti-war demonstrations by radical students in Tōkyō led to
typical pitched street battles against the police in October 1971

have not been confined to such extremists. The *hara-kiri* in 1970 of the
distinguished author, Mishima Yukio, was partly motivated by this
concern, and although initial reactions focused on the sensational aspects of
his action, there are signs that it may eventually prove more significant
than the famous *hara-kiri* of General Nogi. From a slightly different angle,
it is also true that many thoughtful students find it difficult to reconcile
their idealistic education with the patterns of hierarchy and compromise
generally accepted in Japanese society.

Such youthful rebellion is by no means unique to Japan, of course;
however, the form it takes is often distinctively Japanese. In the student
activists' liking for violence and heroic gestures Japanese tradition lives on.
Japanese students still admire the group which makes a hopeless but
symbolic attack on administrative headquarters in the best *samurai* manner
rather than the tactics generally employed by the modernistic Communists of infiltrating boiler-rooms or power plants.

Similarly tradition has lived on in religion, culture and everyday life.
Vast throngs continue to visit temples, shrines and re-built castles; *kabuki*
drama remains popular; outstanding artists and craftsmen are designated

A street in Kanda, the area of Tōkyō which is unequalled in any other
capital in the number of bookshops it contains

'Human National Treasures' and receive official support. It is still not
uncommon to see Japanese women adorned in ceremonial kimonos, while
Japanese men often relax at home in traditional dress; *tatami* matting
remains the usual floor covering and visitors still invariably remove their
shoes when entering a house. Acquaintances still bow to one another and
shop assistants show great deference to customers both in their demeanour
and in the honorific language they employ. Though bread and potatoes
are now quite common, rice remains by far the major item in the Japanese
diet and many of the other foods which Japanese eat are also traditional, as
the foreign visitor, encountering with trepidation objects strange in shape,
colour, smell or taste, often unhappily discovers.

Tradition also continues in more fundamental matters. The hierarchical
group has remained the most important unit in most Japanese lives.
Within the family husbands still receive deferential treatment from their
wives, particularly in front of strangers, even though they normally do not
interfere in the running of the household. Many men spend much of their

leisure time with colleagues from work, generally in bars with attractive hostesses, and the Western pattern of social intercourse and entertainment at home is followed by only a very small minority. Despite this continuation of a certain measure of subservience, however, the evidence from numerous opinion polls suggests that wives have little wish to find new roles outside the home. Although women have entered most areas of public life, the vast majority have been happy to devote themselves to bringing up their children. They do so, in the traditional way, with a marked absence of physical punishment and with boundless attention. Children are privileged persons in Japan and it is common to see them given preference over women, even pregnant women, when there are a limited number of seats available on buses and trains.

The legal jurisdiction of the family-head is now no greater than in Western countries, yet even so most marriages continue to be arranged. It is true that nowadays far more consideration is given to the personal feelings of the young couple, but it is much more common for parents, often still assisted by go-betweens, to introduce to their son or daughter a potential spouse with suitable background, attainments and character, than for marriage to result from a spontaneous romantic attachment. Partly as a result of this pattern women do not marry, on average, until they are in their early twenties and men in their late twenties. Against this, however, it should be stressed that in urban areas most couples now live separately from parents, that wives now have much less fear of their mothers-in-law, and that only fifty per cent of Japanese would regard it as vital to adopt if they had no son to preserve the family line. Nevertheless, that the old-style family is not dead is indicated by the fact that in case of divorce custody of the children is almost as likely to be given to the man as to the woman. For all that female equality is written into the constitution, Japanese women remain subject to traditional patterns to a considerably greater degree than their counterparts in America or Western Europe.

Tradition must therefore enter into any consideration of Japan's future development. While many Japanese intellectuals condemn what they sweepingly term 'the feudal legacy', it is nevertheless arguable that the patterns inherited from the past give hope of continued stability. Factionalism, for instance, will undoubtedly continue to provide checks from within on the abuse of political power, even if governments should manage to manipulate public opinion by making skilful use of the mass media. An even more important tradition, which at last appears to be re-emerging, is nationalism, but it would be wrong to imagine, as some commentators suggest, that this must lead to an aggressive foreign policy. It is quite possible for nationalism to be channelled into pride in Japan's past and present achievements. Japan's most recent history has discredited militarism, and the strength of pacifism since 1945 will make it difficult for any government to arm Japan with nuclear weapons, let alone use them, unless there is a real threat to national security.

Finally, it is important to note the continued strength of the tradition of élite leadership. While the establishment of popular sovereignty has introduced a less authoritarian atmosphere, it has made no great difference in the way in which Japanese government is actually conducted. Since 1952 three élites have controlled Japan—politicians, bureaucrats, and big business. Their relationship has been very close. Politicians depend on *zaibatsu* funds and in return government policy favours business in general and certain companies in particular. Many bureaucrats have enjoyed influential careers in finance and industry after their customary early retirement from public service, and the importance of ex-bureaucrats in politics is illustrated by the fact that almost every post-war Prime Minister in Japan has had a bureaucratic background. These dominant élites have shown themselves to be sufficiently responsive to modern trends to give Japan two decades of skilful administration. If a major world economic crisis were to occur, it is doubtful whether it would shake the foundations of Japanese parliamentary government. Even if it did, the power of the bureaucracy would be unlikely to suffer, and the rise of a demagogic leader with totalitarian ambitions is almost inconceivable.

The bureaucracy provides perhaps the best example of the new blend of modern and traditional which has given post-war Japan much of her economic and institutional strength. Its high standing derives essentially from a technical expertise based on the high educational level of its recruits and intensive study of international conditions, but this is strongly reinforced by a respect for authority fostered by centuries of Confucian teaching.

This combination of old attitudes and new techniques has been a feature of the whole of modern Japanese history, but in pre-war years traditionalism too often played the dominant role. It is because Japan at last appears to have achieved a balanced relationship between traditional and modern attitudes that it is possible to feel confidence about her future.

BOOKS FOR FURTHER READING

ALLEN, G. C., *A Short Economic History of Modern Japan* (Allen & Unwin, London, 1970)

BEASLEY, W. G., *The Modern History of Japan* (Weidenfeld & Nicolson, London, 1963)

DORE, R. P., *City Life in Japan* (Routledge & Kegan Paul, London, 1958)

EMMERSON, J. K., *Arms, Yen and Power* (Tuttle, Tokyo, 1972)

HALL, J. W., *Japan: Prehistory to Modern Times* (Weidenfeld & Nicolson, London, 1970)

IRIYE, A., *Across the Pacific* (Harcourt, Brace, New York, 1967)

JONES, F. C., *Japan's New Order in East Asia: its rise and fall 1937–45* (Oxford University Press, 1954)

NAKANE, C., *Japanese Society* (Weidenfeld & Nicolson, London, 1970)

SANSOM, Sir George, *Japan: A Short Cultural History* (Barrie & Jenkins, London, 1952)

——*The Western World and Japan* (Barrie & Jenkins, London, 1950)

STORRY, R., *A History of Modern Japan* (Penguin Books, Harmondsworth, 1969)

TSUNODA, R. (Editor), *Sources of the Japanese Tradition* (Columbia University Press, 1958)

INDEX

Abe Masahiro, 27, 29
agriculture, post-war, 100–1
Alcock, Rutherford, 32
America, 26–9, 35
American–Japanese relations, 65, 67–8, 84–5
Anglo–Japanese Alliance, the (1902), 44, 68
Army, the Japanese, 58–9, 62, 69–70, 75, 79, 89
artisans, 20
Ashikaga shogunate, the (1338–1573), 11

bakufu, the (*shōgun*'s administrative headquarters, *see also* Kamakura *bakufu*, Tokugawa *bakufu*), 11, 14, 16, 18, 25*ff*
banks, 99
Britain, 26, 28, 29, 32, 39, 40, 65, 81
Buddhism, 10, 22, 56, 103
bummei keika ('civilisation and enlightenment') slogan, 54
Bunraku, 25
bureaucracy, 62–3, 79, 92, 108
bushido ('way of the warrior'), 16

Chiang K'ai-shek, 70, 80, 81
children, treatment of, 107
China Incident, the, 80
Chinese influence, 10
Chōshū 32, 34, 35, 37, 75
Christianity 11, 20, 56, 57
clothing, change in, 53
Communists, 95, 103
company loyalty, 97, 99
Confucianism, 22, 23, 56
conscription, 55

daimyō (feudal lords), 12, 13, 15, 16, 17, 20, 23, 24, 30, 34, 35
Dutch in Japan, 12, 13, 16, 25

'economic miracle', 97

Edo, 15, 20, 32, 35
education, 19, 20, 35, 50, 55–6, 94, 99
élite control, 63, 99, 108
Emperor, 10, 25, 35, 63, 95
Emperor Hirohito, 72, 84, 85, 90, 94
ethics, 55
European influence, 11, 13

factionalism, 75, 103, 107
family system, 23, 24, 50, 51, 57
Fascism, 78–9
feudalism, Japanese, 11, 35, 55
food, 20, 54
foreign advisers, 35, 47
foreign loans, 35, 47
France, 28, 29, 32, 33, 35, 39, 81
fudai daimyō, 15, 27, 29, 32
fukoku-kyohei ('rich country, strong army') slogan, 37, 45, 48
Fukuzawa Yukichi, 42, 55

genrō (elder statesmen), 58–9
geographical factors in Japanese history, 7, 8, 13, 19
Germany, 44, 65, 84
Great Depression, the, 71
Great(er) East Asia Co-Prosperity Sphere, 89
Guadalcanal, Battle of (1942–3), 87

Hamaguchi Yūkō, 61, 69
hambatsu (*han* faction), 39
han (*daimyō* domain), 15, 23, 31, 33
Hara Kei, 59, 61, 67
hara-kiri, 16, 58, 79
Harris, Townsend, 28
Heian (Kyōto), 10
Hideyoshi, *see* Toyotomi Hideyoshi
Hiroshima, 90
Hitotsubashi Keiki, 31–3
Home front, the (during Pacific War), 88, 89

Hotta Masayoshi, 27–9
Hull, Cordell, 85

Ii Naosuke, 29–31
industrial dualism, 101
industrialisation, 45–51
Inukai Ki, 61, 72
Itō Hirobumi, 38, 59
Iwakura Mission, the (1871–3), 35
Iwakura Tomomi, 35, 41

jōi ('expel the barbarian') attitude, importance of in 1860s, 30

Kabuki, 25
Kagoshima, bombardment of (1863), 32
Kamakura *bakufu*, the (1192–1333), 11, 14
kamikaze ('divine wind'), 11, 87
Kanagawa, Treaty of (1854), 27
Katō Kōmei, 61, 65
Katsura Tarō, 59
Kenseikai, the, 61
Kishi Nobusuke, 102–3
Kita Ikki, 74, 77
kobu-gattai ('union of court and military'), 31
Kōdōha, the, 75–7
Konoe Fumimaro, 81, 84–5
Korea, invasion of by Hideyoshi (1592–8), 12–13; Japanese annexation of (1910), 64; Japanese attitudes towards, 40
Kwantung Army, 70
Kyōto, 10, 15, 31

landlords, 18
Land Reform, the (1946), 92, 94, 100
land tax, the, 18, 35, 55
language, the Japanese, 9, 10
legal change, 55, 57
Liberal-Democratic Party, 101–3
'liberal twenties', the, 60–1
literacy, level of in late Tokugawa period, 19
London Naval Treaty, the (1930), 69

MacArthur, General Douglas, 91, 92, 95
Manchukuo, 70
Manchuria, 44, 64, 65, 69, 72

Manchurian Incident, the (1931), 70, 75
marriage, 23, 107
Marxism, 95, 104
Meiji Constitution, the (1889), 38
Meiji (Emperor), the, 33, 58
Meiji Government, the, 33*ff*
Meiji Restoration, the, 31
merchants, 20, 25
Minamoto family, the, 11
Minseitō, the, 61
Mishima Yukio, 105
Mukden, Battle of (1905), 44
Murasaki Shikibu, 10

Nagasaki, 16, 25; atomic devastation of, 90
nationalism, Japanese, 13, 48, 108
Navy, the Japanese, 62, 69, 71, 77, 84, 85, 89
'new religions' in post-war Japan, 103
newspapers, 56, 104
Nisshin Teikei Ron (Japanese–Chinese cooperation argument), 41
Nobunaga, *see* Oda Nobunaga
Nogi, General, 58
Nōhonshugi, 74
Nomonhan, Battle of (1939), 84

Occupation policies, 91–6
Oda Nobunaga, 12
Ōkubo Toshimichi, 33, 37, 40
Ōsaka, 20
oyabun-kobun (parent role–child role) relations, 24–5

Pacific War, the (1941–5), 86–90
Parkes, Sir Harry, 32
Peace Preservation Law (1925), 61
Pearl Harbor, Japanese attack on, 86
peasants, 17–19, 49, 53–4, 71
Perry, Commodore Matthew C., 26
political modernisation, 34–9
political parties, 24, 60–3, 101–4
pollution, 101
population control, 14, 50, 101
Portsmouth, Treaty of, 44
Portuguese in Japan, 11
post-war constitution, the, 94–5

Potsdam Declaration, the (26 July 1945), 90

racial origins, 8
railways, 35, 47, 52
religion, 20–3, 56–7, 103
rice cultivation, 17–18, 100–1
Roches, Léon, 33
Russo–Japanese relations, 42, 65, 71, 84
Russo–Japanese War, the (1904–5), 44, 65

Saigō Takamori, 33
Saionji Kimmochi, 59, 65
sakoku (closed country) policy, 16
samurai: origins of, 10–11; military aware-ness of, 13; ethics of, 16; position in Tokugawa society, 17; discontent of lower *samurai*, 30–1; *samurai* reformers, 34–5; and economic development, 48–9; continuation of *samurai* values, 55
sankin-kōtai (alternate attendance) system, 15, 20
Satō Eisaku, 103
Satsuma, 31–2, 34–5, 37
Security Treaty, the Japanese–American (1952), 96–7, 102
Seiyūkai, the, 39, 59, 61
Sekigahara, Battle of (1600), 13
Sengoku Jidai (Period of Warring Provinces), 11
Shidehara Kijūrō, 68, 70
Shimazu Hisamitsu, 31
Shimonoseki Expedition, the (1864), 32
Shintō, 20–3, 56, 78, 94, 103
shōgun, 14, 25
Shōwa Restoration, the idea of, 72
Siberian Expedition, the, 67
silk, 47, 71
Sino–Japanese relations, 40–2, 64–5, 68, 101
Sino–Japanese War, the (1894–5), 42, 44
Socialists, Japanese, 95–6, 103
Sōka Gakkai, 103
sonno-joi ('revere the Emperor—expel the barbarian') slogan, 29, 31
South Manchuria Railway Company, the, 66, 70

Taika Reform, the (*c.* 646), 10
Taira family, the, 11
'Taishō Democracy', 61
Taishō (Emperor), the, 58
Taishō Political Crisis, the, 59
television, 104
terakoya, 19
Tōjō Hideki, 85, 87
Tokugawa *bakufu* (shogunate), the (1603–1868), 11, 13, 16
Tokugawa heritage and economic change, the, 48–51
Tokugawa Ieyasu, 13–14
Tosa, 33, 35, 37
Tōseiha, the, 76–7
Toyotomi Hideyoshi, 12–13
tozama daimyō, 16, 27
trade unions, 94, 97, 99
tradition, Japanese attitudes towards, 7, 57, 104–7
treaty revision, 39–40
Tripartite Pact, the (1940), 84
Triple Intervention, the (1895), 44
'Twenty-One Demands', the (1915), 65–7

Ultranationalism in pre-war Japan, 62, 72, 74

Versailles Peace Conference, the (1919), 67
village cooperation, 18

war economy, 77–8
wartime atrocities, 80–1
Washington Conference, the (1921–2), 68
Westernisation, 56
women, position of, 24, 94, 106–7
World War I, effects of, 60, 67
World War II and Japan, 81, 84

Yamagata Aritomo, 59, 65
Yamato dynasty, the, 9
Yoritomo (Minamoto Yoritomo), 11
Yoshida Shigeru, 96
Yuan Shih-K'ai, 65, 67

zaibatsu, 71, 79, 94